Heart-Centered Leadership

An Invitation to Lead from the Inside Out

by Susan Steinbrecher and Joel B. Bennett, Ph.D.

BLACK PANTS
PUBLISHING

Memphis, TN

To contact the authors—
Susan Steinbrecher: Susan@instituteofhcl.com
Joel B. Bennett, Ph.D.: Joel@instituteofhcl.com

Copyright©2003 by Susan Steinbrecher and Joel B. Bennett, Ph.D.
Second edition, revised 2004

Published by Black Pants Publishing
158 Perkins Extd.
Memphis, TN 38117

Publisher's Cataloging-in-Publication
(Provided by Quality Books, Inc.)

Steinbrecher, Susan.
    Heart-centered leadership : an invitation to lead
  from the inside out / by Susan Steinbrecher and Joel B.
  Bennett, Ph.D.
  p. cm.
  Includes bibliographical references.
  LCCN 2003109971
  ISBN 0-9703736-1-9

    1. Leadership. 2. Interpersonal relations.
  I. Bennett, Joel B. II. Title

HD57.7.S726 2003   658.4'092
                          QBI03-200688

This book is printed on acid-free paper.

To all those courageous leaders who have
embraced the mission of a more compassionate
and wiser form of leadership.

≈

To my husband, Neal, my lifelong partner, who
has taught me the true meaning of love.

To my teacher and coach, Dr. Dan Mitchell (1945-2004),
who dedicated his life to helping others find their heart.

≈

To my wife, Jan, who ever and always
brings me back to the heart.

To my mother-in-law, Jo Murphy (1934–2004),
who inspired many to live from the heart as she did.

Contents

Acknowledgments

We express our sincere appreciation to all those who provided us encouragement, support, wisdom and inspiration as we embarked on the journey of completing this book. In particular, Harry Bond, Susan Engebrecht, Ruth Ayn Ferguson, Kelly Heath, Pam Long, John Lyden, Don Simonds and Kathleen Wood played an integral part by their willingness to review drafts and provide us with their respectful feedback and wonderful suggestions. This book simply could not have been accomplished had it not been for their dedication and interest in its message. To the entire editing and publishing team—Susan Drake, Lauren Ward, Colleen Wells, Teri Rhodes White, T.J. Greene and Robin Thomas—who were patient with our ignorance of the book publishing process and our extremely busy schedules.

We extend additional thanks to all of our clients with whom we have worked over the years and who have provided us not only with the opportunity to serve them but, more important , their trust and confidence in our work.

Last, to Neal Steinbrecher, Jan Bennett, and our families and friends— your constant support and encouragement meant more than you know at critical times during the writing of this book.

Heart-Centered Leadership: An Invitation to Lead from the Inside Out

Foreword

This is a book on ethics, although the word rarely appears in its pages. In our view, ethics is less about guidelines for the attainment of goodness and is more about your inward, thoughtful strivings toward becoming the best person you can be—for yourself and others. Accordingly, this book is more about process than outcome, more about the journey than the destination, more about your searching for the light than the light itself. To help with that search, we outline specific principles. We suggest you approach each principle as a pointed reminder of the value of personal contemplation rather than some governing precept that should guide your every action. The question to ask is, "How am I proceeding in this path of the heart?" rather than, "Am I there yet?" Similarly, the corresponding virtues should assist you in recognizing particular stirrings within yourself: insights, soulful qualities and emotional purities. These are calling you to keep on the path and to trust the process. This book is an invitation to that calling.

We chose to title this book *Heart-Centered Leadership* to promote a way of leading from the inside out rather than a set of behaviors or competencies. But heart-centered leadership is not a singular gold standard or an ultimate graduation that a rare few can achieve. It lies in your ability to stop, go inward and reflect on the course of action that you know—in your heart— is the right one, rather than succumbing to external pressures and circumstances. As you pay inward attention to the principles and listen to the stirrings of virtue, you will find the most powerful intention is to fully become the best, brightest and most heart-felt leader that you can possibly be. When you do, latch on with all your heart. Then, on any given day, your practice of a principle or demonstration of a virtue will be truly inspirational. Your associates will be happier if you put your heart into your practice than if you look for outward recognition as a leader. This book is an invitation to that practice.

What counts in the end are the people you touch through the purity of your intention and your ability to navigate the dynamics—positive and negative—of commerce and relationships. The invitation to practice is a calling to keep coming from your heart. In our business culture and also in society, the image or metaphor of the heart is often associated with softness, yielding, kindness and—perhaps—weakness. We hope to remind readers that the heart is also strong and powerful, as well as the driving force of life, the vibrant center of circulation. Successful business commerce depends—critically—upon such circulation. We believe that an unbalanced view of the heart underlies at least some of the current crises in business ethics. This book is an invitation to correct that view and create a more ethical business world.

So we have created an invitation at different levels. An invitation to listen, to practice and to change the world by first changing yourself. Our hope is that in time you will accept all three of these. More important, we hope that you will find your own way. For example, you may agree or resonate with some aspects of our message more than others. Also, you will note various references to sentimental, spiritual and religious material; some you may enjoy, others not. Further, you may actively practice all chapter exercises or ignore them altogether. Whatever your preference, we have faith that you will find something to spark your movement on the path of heart-centered leadership. The heart has its ways—many of them.

Your vision will become clear only
when you look into your heart.
Who looks outside, dreams;
Who looks inside, awakens.
—Carl Jung[1]

Introduction
Heart-Centered Leadership

At this very moment—while writing this book—we know we are a work in progress. As much as we will share our personal and professional experiences, we don't have all the answers. We are learning every day about the power of leadership, the power of people, and the power of connecting with people. We want to share with you observations made over the years through our work with clients, friends and associates. We will also share research that provides clear support for the power of people, and the importance of connecting to and adopting a heart-centered leadership style. We know that we have made many mistakes in our own work while leading, managing, supervising, consulting with, and teaching others. We learned, and continue to learn from those mistakes, and hope that we are better leaders today. We also see a great gulf or divide between academic or "book" knowledge about leadership and the real practical lessons that readers like you need to acquire from that book knowledge. We also have a selfish purpose for writing this book, as we believe that the best way to learn lessons is to teach others those lessons. So it is with humble acknowledgment of our own limitations that we begin.

This book is a coordinated effort. Both of us draw from our own personal experiences about the importance of the heart. To best convey this personal message and give flow and coherence to your reading, we will use the pronoun *we* in place of our names. Sometimes the *we* will refer to Susan, sometimes to Joel, but mostly to our common vision to encourage you to embrace a heart-centered leadership style.

Basic Heart Training: What Is Between You and True Leadership?

The message of this book is so simple that it can be summed up in one sentence: True power means listening to and from the heart and having the commitment and humility to clear all that stands in the way of that heart connection.

Of course, this simple message is easier said than done. Humility and selfless commitment to others are not character traits we acquire overnight. Indeed, many people have contrasting or opposing images of leaders: often committed first to achievement for their own selves or careers and to having more pride than humility. This is how it was for Andy Pearson. Pearson is a former CEO of PepsiCo and the founding chairman of Yum! Brands Inc., the firm that manages the fast-food chains of KFC, Pizza Hut and Taco Bell, among others. He was interviewed about his transformation from one of the "ten toughest bosses in America" to a leader with warmth who now sees that his job is to listen to people. "Ultimately," Pearson says, "[leadership] is all about having more genuine concern for the other person. There's a big difference between being tough and being tough-minded. There's an important aspect that has to do with humility. But I've been modestly disappointed at how hard it is to get leaders to act that way. I think it's going to take a generation of pounding away on this theme."[1]

It may not be usual or "normal" for CEOs to demonstrate the virtues of care, concern, warmth and humility in their common dealings with associates. Like trying to squeeze blood out of a turnip, it is often hard "to get leaders to act this way." But will even a generation of pounding away help? Heart-centered leadership follows the path from the inside out—from your values and your passions—rather than from the outside in. We don't prescribe heart-centered leadership. We don't set out a list of actions for you to follow. Nor do we see that the path ahead will be easy. However, we do believe that there is a path, that it is clearly marked, and that anyone can be a heart-centered leader if he or she has the determination and daily commitment to practice certain core principles.

The root or basis of these principles is what we call "the power of the human element." Two things are required to get at and unleash the human element. The first is your ability to listen or—even better—your ability to learn *how* to listen. The second is your own willingness to clear personal obstacles—in other words, your own story and organizational obstacles that get in the way of this deeper listening.

Listening for the Human Element

Heart-centered leadership requires the ability to listen for the human element. Many times when we work with clients, whether conducting a training session or consulting, and especially when coaching executives, we recognize that we are not alone. We aren't alone in that we serve as an instrument through which a crucial message is communicated to the client. This is a message that the client needed to hear from some higher level of wisdom or a higher power. The more we remove our self and our ego from the process, the more the proper words flow, and the exact message that the client was intended to hear is communicated.

Through feedback from the thousands of people with whom we are in contact, both personally and professionally, a common theme has been observed: people want to be valued, cared about, listened to, appreciated, respected, involved and connected. People want to have meaning in their lives. At the very least, they want their self-esteem to be maintained and, ideally, enhanced. Now, even though we observe these needs for value, meaning and self-esteem, it is rare that people verbally express or share them. People at work don't come right out and ask, "Will you value me?" or "How can we create more meaning on the job?" But when we step back and really take in all that is being said—both verbally and nonverbally—we find that, at the root of the problem, frustration or situation, people are really saying that they want to be valued. If you truly listen, and listen at a deeper level, you will see that this need, the "people" need—the human element—is what is being expressed.

Surfacing the Human Element

It is important to understand how the human element shows up at work. Many types of problems result when the needs for self-esteem and meaning are not valued or are even thwarted. The following is a list of ways that the human element surfaces when it does not receive the attention it deserves:

Meetings that drag on. How often do you feel time is wasted in meetings because an associate just wants to be heard or feels that he or she is not valued?

Office politics. When you think about it, office politics are about protection, self-interest and self-esteem; they're about being valued.

Conflicts in our lives. Rarely is the fight or argument about the issue or event we appear to be fighting over. What is it often really about? The person is not feeling good about himself or herself, self-esteem has been lowered, and the individual doesn't feel valued, cared for, appreciated or heard.

Moving and relocation. Businesses often have problems when moving into new office space or relocating associates' offices. Who gets what office and where? Why do people care about this?

Mergers and acquisitions that fail. Failure is often not due to fiscal irresponsibility or lack of due diligence, quite the contrary. Mergers and acquisitions often fail because the leadership team underestimates the impact and the importance of the people factor, indeed, the human element. How will the people in these two or more organizations come together and work together, getting their individual needs met as well as those of the organization? Why should I focus on meeting the needs of my associates? Who is going to make sure that this merger or acquisition is successful? The answer: the people in the organizations.

Hostile associates. Think about the numerous societal issues that filter or bleed into the workplace today. Violence, hostility and employee antagonism are some examples. The associate who shows up to work and shoots his or her manager probably doesn't feel very valued or cared about at work. Of course, one could argue that this individual isn't emotionally stable. However, many, if not most, incidents involving co-worker hostility can be explained to some degree by lack of connection and by social environments that alienate associates.

Sexual harassment. We understand that sexual harassment is less often about sex than about power. Vulgar or lewd comments and inappropriate touching are ways that the harassing person can assert himself or herself. We recognize that at the root of desire for that power lies a deeper need to be valued, respected and cared about.

The need for training in coaching, counseling and discipline. The most-requested workplace training programs are basically about matters of the heart. Many managers need training in coaching, counseling and discipline because they resist or have difficulty communicating with an associate. Many managers have great difficulty conducting a performance-problem discussion in such a way that the associate will respond positively. Associates respond negatively because, in many cases, the manager's primary objective is to punish the associate instead of solving the problem, and the associate senses the manager's lack of respect for him or her. The associate, therefore, takes a defensive stance to protect his or her self-esteem. These managers lose sight of the real purpose of the discussion, which is to motivate an associate to want to change his or her performance. The purpose is not to punish the associate. Effective coaching requires being an adult rather than playing a parental role.

The need for team-building. We've observed that, when a company requests team-building, it is often more about relationships and less about team processes and structures. Leaders want and need their associates to get along, cooperate and get their needs met, both as individuals and as a group. Even when companies request implementation of new teamwork structures, we find that, underneath, leaders hope to better understand the human element and its impact in the workplace. Are we not conducting these sessions so that we begin to build or enhance the relationships in the workplace? Are we not conducting these team-building sessions to ensure that everyone is listened to, valued, appreciated and cared about?

Retention problems. Associates rarely quit the company; they more often quit their boss. For more than 30 years, researchers have studied factors related to associates' commitment to their organizations and their reasons for quitting. Almost always, the number-one determinant of quitting is the lack of leadership or support by administration, managers or supervisors. This finding shows up again and again, across different industries and age groups, and for both men and women.

Lying, cheating and stealing. A recent study by an underwriting company indicates that 56 percent of all associates feel some pressure to act unethically or illegally.[2] Leaders themselves have a profound effect on the ethics of a work culture through their own willingness to follow ethical principles and guidelines.

The need for unions. Why were unions formed in the first place? Because labor typically felt unsupported, uncared about and abused in general. One could argue that the pendulum has swung the other way, with management now feeling that some unions are as controlling as management was when labor organized. Either way, neither party is feeling valued or cared about.

The Human Element and Leadership

The previously mentioned list of factors should convince you of two things. First, there is a great cost when we neglect the human element. Second, a wide variety of problems can be traced back to the human element and also corrected through effort spent in this one area. In short, there is great power in understanding the human element in business. Heart-centered leadership is about your ability to tap into this power. It is about sharing practices, principles and stories that support the notion that the most outstanding leaders understand the power of the human element in business. They understand that businesses are run— and can only be run—by people. They understand that people have the need to be valued, respected, cared about, listened to and involved. And by understanding this, leaders are able to run extremely successful and profitable businesses.

Removing the Barriers

Of course, there are other competencies that factor into a leader's success. But we believe that the human element is at the core, and that both political and business history illustrates this truth. Leadership requires first connecting to, then inspiring, people. It requires removing our own personal and psychological barriers and recognizing, cultivating and maintaining that connection. If each of us uncovers, removes and unveils all the barriers we have put on top of our hearts, we will come from a different place, and our paradigm for relating—the ways we see, approach and work with others—will shift. You see, it is not about learning new skills or competencies. It is about remembering who we are as human beings and letting go of what no longer serves us.

Heart-Centered Leadership: An Invitation to Lead from the Inside Out is not another training program that will teach you all the skills that you need to be a successful leader. We believe you already have what you need to be heart-centered if you are willing to acknowledge and remove all the barriers that are preventing you from ruling from your heart. In general, there are two types of barriers that get in the way of true heart-centered leadership. The first type is our own personal psychology—such as personal stress—fears or lack of confidence; misunderstood or misguided motivations; and outdated, borrowed, preconceived or false notions about leadership. As it has been said, "It's not what you don't know that will cause the greatest problems ... it's what you know that is simply not so." One purpose of this book is to assist you in increasing your willingness to recognize and let go of your own barriers.

The other general type of barrier refers to values and ideals we inherit from the social norms around us, from our institutions and from the culture of the workplace. These include a primary focus on profit at all cost, in addition to: time pressure; the misuse of time and technology; training not to tell the truth and act with integrity; faulty policies and standard operating procedures; or unwritten rules about how to treat fellow associates, business partners and customers.

Take time pressure, for example. Time pressure is very much in the way of heart-centered leadership. In our fast-paced society, some managers e-mail and leave messages for colleagues at times they know those colleagues won't be available to talk. Why would they do that? Because those managers know they don't have enough time to get into a conversation with the individual. They don't really want to take the time to connect because they have so much to do in a day. Also, many executives learn early in their careers that if they want to get to the top, they have to tell some lies along the way. Unfortunately, as they've progressed up the corporate ladder, they have grown so accustomed to telling more and more lies that they forget how to be frank and direct with people in general.

Another purpose of this book is to help you identify barriers to heart-centered leadership that come from your organization, work culture or the way society has helped shape your own career. However, we don't want to put the blame on the business world for these problems. *True heart-centered leadership requires replacing blame with responsibility.* It requires a focused willingness to take responsibility not only for your own personal barriers, but also for all the other barriers. A heart-centered leader recognizes and has compassion for his or her associates, who often are subjected to many stressors, time pressures and ethical problems in the corporate world. The problems that besiege organizations are much better addressed through soul searching, empathy and perspective rather than searching for scapegoats. In our experience, if the leader doesn't clearly see the power of compassionately tapping into the human element, he or she cannot be as successful.

What About Profit?

You may think that a leader who is focused on the human element, on compassion and on removing barriers is a good person, but that he or she just will not cut it in the world of money, competition and a rapidly changing marketplace. The stories and research in this book tell otherwise. For too long we have measured success in an organization by focusing exclusively on profit. Of course, showing a profit is critical to success; at the end of the day, if we don't show a profit, we're not really in business. But who is responsible for showing the profit? Again, it's the people.

We conducted a study for a large publicly traded, hospitality organization that clearly showed the relationship between the internal human element and external metrics of profit. We asked associates from many hotels within the organization what they thought were the most important factors that would make their workplace and work culture positive, excellent and "best of the best." The majority of associates indicated that communication and being listened to by upper management were among the most important. We then asked them how much their particular hotel had these "best of the best" characteristics. We also collected financial data about general operating profit from each hotel. As we expected, those hotels with higher profit margins also tended to be those where the people—the line associates and supervisors—felt that communication was good and that they were respected and listened to.

This finding—based on one company—has been replicated again and again in much larger studies conducted across different types of industries. These studies indicate when associates feel that their organization is a good place to work or has a positive, healthy culture, the company is much more likely to operate at a profit than when associates experience less respect and less heart-centered leadership.

Leaders who were interviewed for this book were asked the question, "What is the role of the leader in an organization?" We were fascinated to discover that not one of them mentioned making money or showing a profit. These leaders recognize that the way to profit is through the human element, through compassion and taking the perspective of those who are doing the day-to-day work. They recognize that money can be made by treating associates with respect and by an ongoing willingness to remove the barriers to connecting. Heart-centered connection is an unquestionable basis for leading organizations to success. Connection is something that just needs to be done.

Is This Book for You?
This book is written for those of you who want to become highly effective leaders—who can achieve extraordinary things for yourselves, your associates and your organizations. You may be struggling because you have gotten the message that compassion doesn't belong in a business environment, while your natural instincts say that it does. You may realize that some of the decisions that you or your organization make may compromise your values and beliefs as a human being. This book is for you if and when you realize that, deep down inside, you and your organization are not doing the right thing for your people, but you are playing the good soldier and carrying on with actions and decisions that supposedly enhance the bottom line. Perhaps you are leaving the workplace with the feeling that there must be a better way. Perhaps you are a first-time leader, or you have not been satisfied either with your own personal results as a leader or

the results of the leaders around you. This book is also for those who have been managing associates for a very long time, but who want to shift not only to a leadership role (there is a difference between management and leadership, as you will soon see), but also to becoming a heart-centered leader. And embracing a heart-centered style requires yet another shift.

What are the differences between a leader and a heart-centered leader? As mentioned above, heart-centered leadership is an inside-out approach, not an outside-in approach. When we are heart-centered, we have the courage to lead with humility and compassion, a relatively unpopular notion in today's business world. Heart-centered leadership means serving those whom you are leading, not the other way around. A heart-centered leader does not "judge" associates' behavior but comes to a place of understanding the behavior. Becoming a heart-centered leader means clarifying your strengths and development needs, and learning who you are and are not as a person—a principle we refer to as "know thyself." A heart-centered leader gives up control because, as leaders, we don't really have it anyway; our associates do. If you think that's not true, try getting anything done without them. Many times people sabotaged the success of their organizations because the associates were not treated well. Heart-centered leadership means understanding that people have positive intentions, even if our associates' behavior appears to illustrate the opposite. Heart-centered leadership means understanding that we as leaders have tremendous impact on the lives of our associates, and that our associates have choices. *At the end of the day, your associates will choose to get on board with you or not.*

This list may sound a bit overwhelming—not what you thought you'd signed up for when you chose a career in leadership. Perhaps the attraction was to be in a power position. By embracing the heart-centered leadership principles, you will be in a more powerful position than you could possibly have imagined. How? What can be more powerful than motivating an associate to do almost anything for you because he or she respects you so highly? What can be more powerful than knowing that you have genuinely and deeply touched the lives of others by your actions? What can be more powerful than having an associate who, after working for you, chooses to model himself or herself after your leadership style? The leaders profiled in this book have achieved all of this. They continue to have a significant impact on the lives of hundreds of people and are successful by all counts—including producing positive financial results for their organizations. Many of these leaders are not famous or well known in the public domain, but to the associates who work with them, they are heroes.

Ultimately, this book is about learning how to make a difference. In the final analysis, we want to help those of you who really want to make a difference, a real contribution not only in your own life, but also certainly in the lives of your associates and possibly society as a whole.

Exercises

At the end of every chapter, we give you the opportunity to reflect upon the ideas or principles discussed. These exercises will be in the form of questions, a brief survey or some suggestion for action. In order to receive the full benefit of this book, we strongly recommend taking a few moments to contemplate the exercise. Do what you can to set aside 10 minutes: close the door, turn off the phone, move away from the computer, find a relaxing chair. Do something that symbolizes to you that you are *stopping* your external activity and making the commitment to work "from the inside out." Because the exercises in each chapter build on those from the preceding chapters, we recommend that you buy a journal in which to record them. Keep your answers to these questions with you until you have finished reading this book.

1. When was the last time you *really listened* to someone *when it was difficult* for you to do so? You can choose an experience from either your work or personal/home life. By "difficult" we mean listening to someone who did not agree with you, or listening

when you did not have the time to listen, or listening to someone who was bringing bad news, judging you, or was otherwise an irritation. As you recall the experience, write down your answers to these questions:

- Why was it difficult?
- What were you feeling?
- What did you want to do instead of listening?
- How did you show that you were listening?
- How did you show that you were not listening?
- What underlying message did you give the other person?
- What was the outcome of the communication?

As you recall this experience, reflect on those qualities within yourself that represent your "barriers"—that is, reflect on the resistance or distractions within yourself that keep you from doing a better job of listening with a sense of care and concern for others. Write down all those characteristics that come to mind, or the situations and circumstances in which you exhibited them. (Note: As you write this and other personal inventory lists, please remember to proceed slowly and be kind to yourself.)

2. Now reflect on your organization's barriers to listening. Again, write down whatever comes to mind. You may use both your current and previous business settings.

3. After—only after—you have made both of these lists, take a look at them side by side. Reflect on whatever similarities you see in these lists. For example, is one longer than the other? Why? Are there clear parallels between the two? Is there a

common theme represented in both lists? Two or more common themes? How do you feel looking at each list? Are the feelings different?

Chapter 1

From Management to Leadership and
Heart-Centered Leadership

Imagine it is the end of your professional career and you are about to retire. You have been fortunate to work for an organization long enough to collect a substantial pension. So you will retire in comfort and security. You have also worked in various positions with a great number of people and have overcome tremendous challenges. The organization is very appreciative of all your efforts and contributions and throws you a retirement party. It is the night of the retirement party. The room is beautiful and elegantly appointed. The band is playing in the background. The bars are well-equipped with the best brands and the food is sensational. You are especially happy that all the important people in your life are present. It is a magical evening that you will never forget. The emcee wishes to propose a toast. Which of the following toasts do you want the emcee to propose?

1. "[Your name] was a wonderful manager. He or she did an outstanding job over the years keeping our costs in line, balancing the budget and showing a profit year after year. [Your name] was particularly good at planning, controlling costs and organizing. Indeed, [your name] helped set the standard for using well-established solutions to overcome problems. Ladies and gentlemen, please put your hands together to show your appreciation for [your name]."

2. "What an inspiring and motivating leader [your name] was during [his or her] many years of employment with us! We all know that [your name] has that special gift for encouraging people do to their best. And this includes not only those of us gathered here tonight, but also the many who came in contact

with [him or her]. As you look around the room, you can see the impact that [he or she] has made on so many lives. Through [your name]'s inspiration and efforts, we have realized many years of success and have taken a leading position in the industry. Ladies and gentlemen, please put your hands together to show your appreciation for [your name]."

3. "Tonight we honor [your name] for [his or her] leadership in taking this company to a premier position in the industry. But, more than this, [your name] has personally if not deeply touched every person in this room. We all have stories of how [your name] went out on a limb for an associate or helped us out of a jam. I would like to speak personally about this. I remember when [your name] pulled me aside and asked me about what was happening in my life. I thought that [your name] wanted to talk to me because my performance had clearly slipped. But [your name] never addressed my performance; you just asked me how I was doing. As some of you know, I was going through a very difficult time, having learned that my wife had cancer—and, of course, this affected my work. But [your name] somehow never 'talked work'—[your name] trusted me. The care and support that [your name] gave touched me deeply, and my wife and son were also personally grateful. Because of your heartfelt support, I wanted to work harder not to let you down, even in the midst of a personal crisis. As you all know, I was able to turn my performance around. As you also know, my wife passed away several months later. I will never forget the kindness and compassion that [your name] showed for me during that time. I will never forget [your name]. I can only hope that one day I can exemplify the type of leader that [your name] was to us all."

So which toast would you prefer to receive? We emphasize that any one you choose is correct; there is no wrong answer. Indeed, it is possible that all three appealed to you for different reasons. This exercise is designed to encourage you to take a look at where you are going in the long run—or time horizon—of your life. In fact, your ability to do this—to take the broad perspective—is a quality this book asks you to cultivate. In other words, your choice of toast is less important than the process you go through in discerning which one fits your own long-term goals. This process of discernment is what heart-centered leadership is all about. Consider the following interpretations of each of the above toasts.

The first scenario describes the success of an excellent, thorough and accomplished manager. This type of individual is a necessary and vital asset to any organization, because he or she keeps things running, makes ends meet and helps to turn a profit. Choosing this first toast suggests that you value good work, achievement and also the ability to master the task of juggling people, profit and customers.

The second scenario depicts the achievements of good leadership—someone who not only helped to make the organization successful but has also motivated and inspired people to keep that success going. This type of individual helps make the organization not only profitable, but also a good—and perhaps "great"—place to work. Such leaders inspire associates to help bring their companies through difficult times. If you chose this second toast, you likely have the desire to show respect for associates and customers, to motivate all associates to do their best, and to strike a balance among improving customer service, supporting associates and turning a profit.

The third toast depicts a different type of leader: someone who places great importance on the personal needs of people. Such leadership is not as concerned with external success as it is about the precedent of people, creating win-win situations wherever possible, and trusting that "putting relationships first" will result in a deeper type of success that cannot be measured in terms of profit. This type of leader gives associates not only a sense of purpose, but also a feeling of care, concern and connection. Such leaders bring companies through difficult times *because* they help people during their own personal difficult times. Choosing this third toast indicates that you have a great trust in the power of people and their ability to transform themselves. You are likely motivated by the wonder and power of such transformation, and experience tells you that high-quality service and financial success will follow.

Regardless of which toast you chose, we believe that this book will assist you on your road to heart-centered leadership. You may *believe* that it is not always possible or appropriate to lead in a heart-centered way and that it is sometimes necessary to be a manager and a leader. However, as you read on, *you will discover that it is quite often necessary to be a heart-centered leader at a moment's notice.* In other words, we wrote this book as *an invitation to lead in a different way;* a way that requires great courage but will yield outstanding results for you personally and for your organization in the long run. We ask you to develop your God-given capacity to lead with compassion and authenticity. Not only is this ethically the right thing to do, but we also believe that heart-centered leadership will become more and more necessary for organizations to survive. Let us tell you why.

In the past, leadership was simpler. Yesterday's leaders could demand performance. But today's leaders must also contend with two very important factors: *complexity and tight resources.* The manager in the first scenario is a top-of-the-line performer, and—if you go this route—you are likely to achieve success. But today's leaders are faced with a much more educated and democratically oriented workforce, for whom success has many meanings. The business issues of today are much more complex and go beyond performance. They require adapting, building networks and dealing with: rapidly changing, multistructured, matrixed or flattened lines of reporting, as well as intranets, virtual meetings, 24/7 work weeks and outsourced, downsized and mobile functions.

The leader in the second scenario understands this complexity and is able to balance profit and customer satisfaction with the need to support associates. But the leader of today is also expected to do more with fewer resources in half the time. As a result, today's leader must have the ability to encourage and apply the ideas, creativity and contributions of all the organization's human resources. Most important, he or she needs to be able to connect with, respect and show value to associates—amidst the time pressures and limited resources. This is why the leader in the third scenario will become more and more necessary.

The three scenarios offer quick summaries of this chapter's main ideas. They distinguish among a manager of excellence, a great leader and a heart-centered leader. They also show the three core factors that each of these roles must work: associates, customers and profit. (For a complete understanding of these three factors, refer to the discussion and Figure 1.4 on page 39.) The manager performs by juggling these three factors. The leader inspires by balancing them and aligning associates with a common vision. The heart-centered leader connects and touches associates; as a result, customers are served and profit is sustained, if not increased.

To meet future challenges, you need all three types of managers/leaders in your organization. But, most important, you need the involvement and commitment of every associate, not only to find solutions but also to implement the solutions effectively. You need to know those with whom you are working and from what perspective you are approaching them. In this chapter, we explore the differences between management and leadership.

Heart-Centered Leadership Is Necessary for Organizational Health
(Research Note)

Academic and real-world research suggests that heart-centered leadership is associated with a variety of critical success factors, including greater financial health. In one study, the most financially successful companies had leaders with the same heart-centered qualities we outline in later chapters: humility, self-honesty and open-mindedness. In another study, the more profitable companies had leaders who were very sensitive to the impact they had on others. Other research on the effectiveness of United States presidents suggests they were able to balance their strong drive to influence others with a willingness to set aside personal goals. This and other research indicates that heart-centered leadership is not just some nice idea or theory or some magical dream. Rather, as businesses grow and the speed of commerce increases, the core virtues of heart-centered leadership will become increasingly necessary. Such leaders will have greater ability to meet the complexities of multiple partnerships and the cooperative business landscape of the future, while maintaining integrity and identity of their own organizations.[1]

We then further investigate differences between leadership and heart-centered leadership, the latter being the focus of this book.

Manager, Leader, Heart-Centered Leader

So what is management versus leadership versus heart-centered leadership? There are many ways to distinguish the three, and we offer the following as only one possibility. Please also review Figure 1.1 on the following page.

We define management as the following:
Management is the process of working through others to achieve organizational objectives in a changing environment. This entails the effective and efficient use of limited resources.

And we would define leadership as the following:
Leadership is the ability to make things happen by encouraging and inspiring others and acting as a catalyst for change.

And heart-centered leadership is defined as the following:
Having the wisdom, courage and compassion to lead others with authenticity, humility and service.

So what are the key differences among these three? Do you notice that you get a different feeling from each of these definitions? What feeling do you get with the management definition? What feeling do you get with the leadership definition? What about the heart-centered leadership definition?

When we ask clients this question in workshops or in coaching, the answers are typically the same. They say that the management definition has a feeling of someone being efficient, effective, disciplined and orderly. The leadership definition evokes a feeling of someone creating a vision and rallying others, influencing and inspiring them to achieve that vision. The heart-centered leadership definition evokes a feeling of spirituality, courage, humility and greatness; the courage to tackle the problems of the organization with truth and care; and the drive to never settle for less than the best. Look

	Management	Leadership	Heart-Centered Leadership
Approach to problems	More scientific	Fewer explicit tools	Wisdom and intuition
Approach to people	More formal	Requires eliciting teamwork and cooperation from a vast network of people and motivating people in that network	Believes that, given the right support, people rise to the occasion on their own and enjoy being held accountable
Beliefs about how to influence others	Relies on the foundational skills, such as planning, controlling and organizing	Frequently displays enthusiasm, passion, and inspiration to get others to attain levels	Models authenticity of performance (walking the talk), commitment to personal and others' well-being and faith that others will do the right thing
Beliefs about change	Based on reasoning process and testing (try out what worked in the past)	Makes use of his or her imagination and creativity to bring about change; seeks to master the change process	Believes that change process occurs through living certain principles; trusts the process of change through relationships
Emotional style	Involves less outward emotion	Shows enthusiasm for vision, goals and purpose.	Openly shows emotion and makes it safe for others to show emotion
Personality at work	More conservative demeanor to achieve goals	More often a liberal demeanor or strong "personality"	Personality may or may not be in the foreground; style is flexible
Key contribution	Implementing the vision	Creating a vision	Leading with vision, humbleness, love and compassion
Orientation to service, associates and profitability	Juggle	Balance and align	Care, connect and enrich
Key motives	Control	Power and influence	Guided by ethical, moral, or spiritual values (e.g., authenticity, compassion)

Figure 1.1

at the differences among managing, leading and heart-centered leadership listed in Figure 1.1 on the preceding page.

As you can see, there are vast differences among management, leadership and heart-centered leadership. Don't misunderstand—good solid management is critical to an organization's success, so you either have these skills or you need to surround yourself with these skills. But to lead your organization effectively in the future, you have to combine management, leadership and heart-centered leadership skills on your team.

Embracing Key Principles

How do these leadership skills differ from the skills of a heart-centered leader? Heart-centered leadership encompasses all of the above leadership skills and takes the next step into a more powerful dimension. This more powerful dimension produces a leader who leads from principles, values and virtues. Principles can be defined as rules or codes of conduct. This book introduces some key guidelines for behavior. But in order for this behavior to be heart-centered, authentic and real, it has to come from a place of emotional resonance and coherence. You have to believe in what you are doing. It has to resonate with you. So for each of the principles we discuss, we also talk about an internal virtue or emotional state that brings coherence to what you are doing. The seven principles and corresponding virtues are:

Principle	Virtue
Know thyself	Commitment to personal growth
Don't judge, don't assume; instead, come to understand	Open-minded
They need what you need	Authenticity
Letting go	Detachment
Know the impact of your words and actions	Integrity/foresight
Associates have a choice; they ultimately will decide to go along or not	Humility/humbleness
Care for the heart	Self-care/emotional health

Figure 1.2

As stated earlier, we are not here to teach a certain set of skills or preach a fixed set of behaviors. Rather, we hope to give you a clear sense about a certain way of being and living. Principles relate to conviction, and a deep and abiding belief in the nature of work and people. They are about living with integrity and honesty, and using certain ideas as a code or basic tenet about how to behave. For example, consider the following affirmation:

Who I am and my ability to act with truthfulness and integrity
are more important than my achieving success.[2]

We came across this affirmation while struggling to understand why a certain project was not getting done and why associates were not meeting deadlines. By willingly putting aside our own expectations and focusing more on living in a principled way, we actually made more room for the associates to get the work done. Because affirmations can be an important tool for living the seven principles, these and other positive statements will be shared throughout this book. Understanding and embracing the seven principles will take you from where you are today to being heart-centered.

Certainly when we think of leaders, many great military figures come to mind: Julius Caesar, Attila the Hun, Alexander the Great, Napoleon Bonaparte, General George Patton. Indeed, entire books have been written about how managers can lead like these figures. General Patton, perhaps the toughest of them all, successfully mustered the troops into battle by barking orders in World War II. We think of many of these leaders as hard core, making tough decisions, inciting followers to win against insurmountable odds and sometimes browbeating people into subservience. Those tactics were successful in their times and under certain circumstances.

In many ways, times have changed, and our workforce has changed with them. All research on Generations X and Y indicates that the workforce longs for a more connected, supportive family environment in which personal needs are met along with those of the organization. Our current workforce wants to be involved and part of the decision-making process.

In some ways, other types of leaders come to mind when we think of ways to create a more connected workplace: Mahatma Gandhi, Nelson Mandela and Abraham Lincoln provide some examples.

To further illustrate this point, let's do an exercise. Take a pencil and your journal, and make two lists—one titled "SAY/DO" and the other titled "IMPACT." Think about the best boss for whom you ever worked. This is the boss for whom you had tremendous respect and would do anything within reason. If this boss called you in on your day off, you would be there for him or her in a "New York minute"—that is how strongly you feel about this person. Now, thinking of this individual, describe all the things this person would say or do: in other words, his or her behaviors that caused you to think of him or her as your best boss. It is most helpful if you write this list down, taking a few minutes to think while you make the list. Now that you have a good list of words and behaviors, think of the resulting impact this person had on you and record this under "IMPACT."

Once you have completed this exercise, do the same with the worst boss for whom you ever worked. If this boss called you in on your day off, you wouldn't even answer the phone. Again, list the things this person said or did, the behaviors that caused you to think of him or her as your worst boss. Again, describe the impact this boss had on you.

So what behaviors are on your best-boss list? Did you list things such as great planner, organizer, knew how to make money, turn-around artist? In our work as facilitators, we have conducted this exercise with 100 different groups representing managers and leaders from every imaginable position and occupation. We have never had a person say that his or her best boss was a great planner, terrific organizer, "she knew how to make a profit," "he gave us the best benefits," etc. (which would be viewed as more management-type skills). Instead, the list on page 37 is more typical:

Best Boss	
Say/Do	Impact
Listened to me	Motivated me
Genuinely cared about me	Made me want to do my best
Made time for me	I wanted to be that type of leader
Gave me feedback	Inspired me
Trusted me to make the decision; didn't make it for me; empowered me	I felt more confident and competent with the decisions I had to make
Involved me	Made me feel good about myself
Worst Boss	
Say/Do	Impact
Took credit for my work	Created tremendous stress and resentment
Threatening and blaming style	I quit
I received no feedback	I stayed physically, but left mentally
Screamer, intimidated everyone around	Called in sick a lot
Favored some employees over others; not fair	My motivation to do well was lessened; had a lack of trust for the boss

Figure 1.3

So what can we conclude from this exercise? Would you say that these behaviors represent more of a management role or a leadership role? Again, in conducting this exercise at least 100 times, we never saw the typical management competencies listed. You may have noted that the exercise leaves it completely open for someone to respond in any way he or she sees fit. It asks participants to tell about their best and worst boss. It doesn't coach you to tell about your most motivating or inspiring boss. It completely leaves it up to you (and those 100 groups of managers) to put down what comes to mind. So how is it possible that things such as good planner, organizer, and profit-maker aren't hitting the list? Do these "best boss" leaders not have these skills? Or do they have these skills but these are not the ones which come to mind when associates are asked, "Who is your best boss?"

When groups shared their list of behaviors, we also asked them whether their best bosses had typical manager competencies as well; most of the time the response was affirmative. So if that is the case, why didn't respondents put those behaviors and competencies on the list? The reason is that, at the end of the day, these bosses touched the hearts of these group members.

They inspired them, influenced them and made an impact on them forever. "Forever?," you ask. And how much of an impact? When these participants were asked to share how long ago they had worked for this best boss, it was not uncommon to hear that they worked for this boss 4 to 25 years ago. They worked for this boss 25 years ago! That is making an impact on an individual. And we will also tell you that when asked to come up with this best boss, managers and leaders often identified this best boss within 15 to 20 seconds! Now that is making an impact.

> Our best bosses listened to us, believed in us, cared about us as people, made time for us. They involved us and knew that we, as human beings, want to be a part of something great. Therefore, they influenced, inspired and motivated us.

Leaders like Angie Mock and Perry Sorenson truly understand this. When Angie Mock started her new company, Flagstone Hospitality Management, she brought in associates at all levels of the organization from 50 hotels and asked them to help create a set of company values. Angie understood that, in order for the associates to embrace, buy into and commit to living the organization's values, the values had to be generated by them. This group agreed on seven key values that would guide them in everything they did.

Perry Sorenson, COO of Outrigger Hotels & Resorts, had a similar approach. Outrigger experienced a significant downturn in the marketplace. Specifically, it went from a 90 percent demand to a 60 percent demand. Perry realized that the organization had to do something immediately. Perry took this opportunity to look at the company. He wanted to understand what the organization stood for and why people came to Hawaii to stay with them. To do this, he began by trying to determine why their associates worked for them. Why were they not working for their competitors? Perry discovered that his associates really embodied the spirit of Hawaii and the spirit of hospitality. In Perry's words, "We started a process, first of all, making sure that all of our people understood the tradition of Hawaii. We wanted them to feel a part of the community. We went to our associates and asked them some questions. We asked, 'When we are operating at our best, what are we doing? What are our values? What is precious to us?' From these discussions, we created our values, all associate-driven, not management-driven."

These two examples show that heart-centered leaders do not seek input from associates just for show. They don't just act like they care about their associates viewpoint because they read in some management book that this is an important part of a good leader. Rather, heart-centered leaders make time because that is what their hearts tell them to do ... "put people first." Heart-centered leaders like Angie Mock and Perry Sorenson develop strategies that involve, promote, call upon and inspire associates to participate fully in creating, renewing or revitalizing the organization. They do this with care, compassion and empowerment.

Management, Leadership, and Heart-Centered Leadership

There are many ways to help you distinguish whether you are operating as a manager, leader or a heart-centered leader. The idea is for you to explore which of these three models you are drawn to, and also to notice when and why you work in any of the roles. It is possible that in any given day, you spend some time as a manager, some time as a leader and some time as a heart-centered leader. There are two ways to look at these distinctions. The first deals with your orientation to customers, associates and profits. Look at the following diagram.

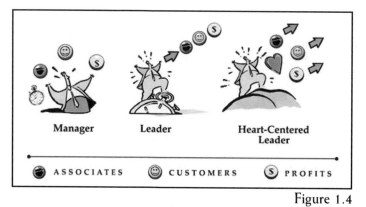

Figure 1.4

Anyone in a management or leadership position has to get associates to be productive to make customers happy and ultimately to make money. As we see it, effective managers often are made so by their *ability to juggle* these three factors. Some moments they put associates first; other times they put customers first and sometimes profits first. It all depends upon timing and the importance of *meeting goals within certain structures* (policies/standard operating procedures) and *time frames.* Effective leaders, on the other hand, *start with a vision,* and usually (although not always), start by *aligning associates with this vision.* Associates, in turn, realize this vision by improving customer satisfaction. The ultimate result is increased business and profits. Leaders still have to be aware of goals, structures and time frames, but they do whatever it takes to *inspire associates to use or leverage goals and structure in order to make the customer happy.*

The heart-centered leader puts emphasis on whatever is needed to connect with associates in a caring and compassionate manner, while understanding the resources and constraints of goals and structures. However, heart-centered leaders are willing to let go of (or put aside) certain policies and timelines to honor, respect and care for associate relationships, as well as their own health and well-being. This does not mean that policies and procedures fall apart or are neglected. Rather, the heart-centered leader has complete faith in the power of people, and rests his or her work on this faith. Through this faith in the heart—and one's own heart space—there is a simultaneous or synchronistic increase in productivity, customer service and profits. No one is more important than the other, and the leader is very involved and part of the process.

The second way to understand differences among management, leadership and heart-centered leadership deals with influence, power and control. Let's review our definition of management: *Management is the process of working through others to achieve organizational objectives in a changing environment. This entails the effective and efficient use of limited resources.*

Managers often get their power through an organizational chart—by virtue of their position. Achievement is a key (if not *the* key) goal for managers. In order to achieve, managers must influence people; they often or almost always do so by virtue of the power they hold as managers. In other words, effective managers exercise some degree of influence and power, and that helps them work through and with others to achieve organizational goals. In addition, managers are aware that they have limited resources (supplies, materials, time, money, staff, etc.). Thus, they also have to exercise some control so these resources are not wasted and, more important, are used in ways that reduce costs and increase profits. Effective managers use control (through policies and procedures) to maximize success. This is one reason we see managers as jugglers; they have to keep resources at hand and ensure that associates use them wisely.

Leaders also have power, influence and control, but in an entirely different way. While managers most often get power by virtue of their position, leaders have power by virtue of their passion and who they are. Followers ascribe or hand real power to leaders; a leader's power doesn't come through organization charts. It's possible to be a real leader, whether or not you are in a position of power. Let's compare two types of associates to help explain this idea:

> **Associate #1** often gets the job done, follows the rules and maintains productivity, but never feels inspired by work or has a sense of the bigger picture or purpose of the organization. Imagine that this first associate has a good manager who makes sure resources are used correctly and communicates regularly with the associate to see that goals are being met.

> **Associate #2** is similarly a productive and good worker who also goes the extra mile, comes up with new ideas and seeks ways to improve things. Imagine that this second associate knows a line-level supervisor from another work crew—someone who listens to him and motivates him, someone who "leads" him. Indeed, this supervisor has very little position power and, formally speaking, is not in a *position* of leadership. Instead, he is able to persuade, inspire, share good ideas and motivate others. In short, his influence leads associates to look up to him, and, in a way, the associates give that supervisor some power in their work lives.

Recall the definition of leadership: *the ability to make things happen by encouraging and inspiring others, and acting as a catalyst for change.*

You will notice that leadership focuses more on the *ability to influence,* whereas management deals more with the *technical process of getting things accomplished.* People (associates, employees, subordinates) are involved in both cases, but the meaning of "people" is entirely different. Management always involves the element of *control* when it comes to people. It is more often necessary for managers to control than for leaders to control. For leaders, people are meaningful not in that they *can be* influenced, but in *how they are* influenced. Leaders are more adept at knowing when such influence is soft or hard. Soft influence comes by encouraging, suggesting, consulting, inspiring, cheering, reassuring and exciting. Hard influence comes through pressuring, setting firm goals, laying down a challenge, enforcing, insisting, compelling or urging. A leader's ability to influence requires versatility in these skills, whereas managers generally are less concerned with *inspiring* associates as long as the job gets done.

Heart-centered leadership is entirely different when it comes to power, influence and control. The issue is not how or whether associates are inspired or how the job gets done; the issue is how the leader *can best serve* his or her associates. Recall the definition of true power from the introduction: *True power means listening to and from the heart, and having the commitment and humility to clear all that stands in the way of that heart connection.*

As we shall see in later chapters, heart-centered leadership is about a deeper kind of power—some may call it a transcendent or spiritual power. You decide what that source of power is or how you name it. We only wish to offer other ways of understanding the distinction among management, leadership and heart-centered leadership.

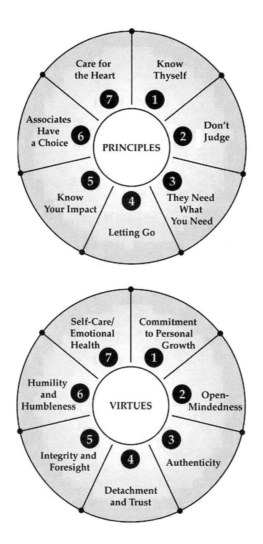

Figure 1.5 The Seven Core Principles and Virtues of Heart-Centered Leadership.
The following chapters of this book explore the seven principles and their corresponding virtues, shown in the above diagrams. As you read through this book and work with different exercises, you will come to understand your own strengths and identify areas that need work. On any given day, you can use these diagrams as a tool to help you identify which principle you will work on improving that day.

Chapter 2
Know Thyself (Your Commitment to Personal Growth)

Why do you see the speck in your neighbor's eye but do not notice the log in your own eye?
Or, how can you say to your neighbor, "Let me take the speck out of your eye,"
while the log is in your own eye? First take the log out of your own eye, and then
you will see clearly to take the speck out of your neighbor's eye.
—Matthew 7:3–5 NRSV

Not the faults of others nor their errors of commission or omission,
but one's own errors and omissions should the sage consider.
—Buddha

Happy is the person who finds fault with himself instead of finding fault with others.
—Islamic Saying

What is the difference between a good leader and a heart-centered leader? First and foremost is the willingness to look in the mirror. In other words, come to understand who you are, and therefore "know thyself." When you know who you are, you can begin to master the art of leading yourself and therefore will model a way for your associates to do the same. Consider the above passages from three major world religions.

What do these passages suggest? If you want to lead others—that is, show them how to improve—then take a good look in the mirror first. To be a heart-centered leader means being willing to examine yourself. This is a very difficult task! We are accustomed to talking about the faults of others without asking ourselves these questions: "What part do I play in this situation? How do my actions contribute to the problem?"

Knowing and Showing Our Humanity
There is an ancient tale about Moses, a great leader who helped free the Israelites from bondage and slavery in Egypt. The king of Egypt, the great Pharaoh, wanted to understand why and how Moses was having such a strong

influence on the Israelites. How could Moses be such a great leader? Pharaoh commissioned his artists to study Moses by painting pictures of him. These were special court artists whose paintings were used to understand the inner personalities or central selves of their portrait subjects.

When the artists returned with their renderings of Moses, the Pharaoh was upset and confused. They had drawn a somewhat ugly face covered with scars, sores and disfiguring blemishes. Pharaoh asked his wizard artists, "How can this be? How can a man who looks like this be seen by others as such a great leader?" The artists explained that the face of Moses showed that he was not afraid to hide anything about his basic human frailties, that he was honest about all that he was on the inside, that he was aware of his own defects or character flaws, and that he was willing to persevere for the freedom of his people—a freedom that transcended his humanness.

In other words, the Israelites saw someone very human, someone they could trust and someone who embodied the spirit of truth. Moses was not focused on others' problems, but, through spiritual effort, was able to work out his own problems rather than keep them hidden from others. Indeed, there is an important relationship among how we relate to—and accept—our own inner (and very human) flaws and how much we focus on the problems of others. In general, the more energy we spend on blaming others, the less willing we are to look at, examine and work on our contribution to the problem. Conversely, the more we "clean up our side of the street," the more energy we will have to work through problems with others.

To be clear, this focus on one's flaws is not an end in itself. Many of the leaders we interviewed for this book emphasize the importance of looking in the mirror in terms of improving their relationships. Their self-reflection involves a deliberate effort to review the talents and skills as well as the personal stresses of their associates. That is, heart-centered leaders pursue self-knowledge as much for self-improvement as for the enhancement of their associates and the overall betterment of their organizations. Antoinette Samuel, who is Executive Director of the American Society for Public Administration and recent CEO of the Employee Assistance Professionals Association, put it this way:

I do a lot of reflection, reassess the decisions I have made every day on the long trip home. I am my own worst critic; I question myself again and again. I review my actions to see how they contributed to the outcome. But the outcome is not as important as the road I took—in my relationships with people—that contributed to the outcome. Did I do anything unethical? Did I exercise poor judgment? Did I do or say anything that may have adversely affected someone? To really lead, I also have to observe my associates and how they work, how they contribute; and this takes time. I take a lot of time to think about and reflect about how their natural talents and skills relate to the goals of the organization. I make it relevant to work and then somehow make the connection for them. You have to take the time to know people. You have to help them recognize talents that they have and that they may have never recognized in themselves. As they do, and as they express them, then over time, they see the workplace as a totality of experience; leadership is part of that totality.

One heart-centered outcome of self-reflection is what Antoinette calls "synergy." This involves a realization for both you and your associates that you are there together at a deeper level of self-expression. You find ways to give people the opportunity to express who they really are—their natural skills and talents—through their work. At the same time, they experience you as leading them toward that self-expression as a way of contributing to the organization. The key to all this is first taking a look at yourself.

We Have Met the Enemy, and They Are Us

Often we are so focused on what is wrong with others that we don't look at ourselves. Yet who determines the direction of an organization, a department, a team or even a small work group? Ultimately, we do. We once facilitated a retreat for senior-level executives from a major organization. We were baffled to hear them say things like, "They won't allow us to move forward here and do what this organization needs" and "They are not supporting us." After listening to these complaints for a while, it was necessary to clarify what "they" meant. We simply asked, "Ladies and gentlemen, who are THEY? We are under the impression that this team is the most senior-level team in the organization. Are we mistaken?" There was dead silence. You could have heard a pin drop in the room. Why? Because the senior team realized that they had been looking outside of themselves to pin blame for the organization's problems when in fact, they themselves were the ones responsible for the organization. And the entire organization counted on them for leadership. This group of executives finally came to terms with the fact that they were "they."

In our executive coaching practice, we frequently run into this problem of external focus. Sometimes executives request coaching because they are beginning to derail in their careers, and they know something has to change. All the competencies and attributes that have gotten them where they are today no longer work, or simply are not enough anymore. It is common for clients to have little awareness of their leadership style and the impact that this style has on others. Not only are they unaware of who they are, but in some cases, they are unwilling to explore themselves. Leaders who are unwilling to look in the mirror, to "know thyself," typically don't last. These are the leaders who ultimately end up firing themselves.

Why is it so difficult to look at ourselves? Of what are we afraid—that we will see something we don't like? Perhaps. However, a heart-centered leader recognizes that this is a critical step. Sharon Wibben, senior vice president of in-flight service for Delta Air Lines, probably said it best: "How can we ask other people to empower themselves when we are not self-empowered?" When we put all our energy into figuring out what is wrong with others, we disempower ourselves. Think about it. When was the last time you succeeded in changing another person? If a person chooses to change, it is because he or she decides to do so. We tend to focus on others' shortcomings and become blind to our own. Heart-centered leadership requires sincere willingness to first look in the mirror and examine ourselves.

Changing Our Bosses

Dealing with our own bosses provides a good and common example of how difficult it is to self-examine, and also shows how heart-centered leadership can come from an associate to his or her own boss. One woman, we'll call her Melanie, sought advice from us on how to deliver corrective feedback to her boss, John. Melanie was experiencing much stress and concern about problems stemming from John's unwillingness to change. Whenever a boss, or anyone else for that matter, is not aware of his or her behavior, such corrective feedback can be helpful, providing it is offered in a loving, heartfelt manner. In this case, John had already received feedback from all of his associates. So we asked Melanie, "Do you think John already knows how his behavior is affecting you and the others around him?" Now, of course, the answer to that question was yes, but it was important for Melanie to discover this for herself. After Melanie answered affirmatively, we proceeded to ask her, "For what purpose, then, would you provide John feedback that he has already received numerous times, since he is aware of this behavior?" Melanie responded, "But John has to change!"

Then we asked Melanie, "When was the last time you were successful in changing someone?" Of course, Melanie admitted she had never been successful in changing anyone. We agreed with Melanie that the first step is to provide a person with feedback about how his or her behavior is affecting others; but, since John had received this feedback already, this was not the best approach. We helped her to understand that John obviously had made a decision not to change, since he had already received a tremendous amount of feedback on his behavior.

Melanie eventually understood the importance of letting go and honoring John's decision not to change. Even when we care deeply about our boss and are convinced that change would serve his or her best interests, we must recognize that it is only our own opinion. With this recognition, Melanie realized that the only person that she could change was herself, and also that she could change her behavior toward John. We discussed with Melanie the possibility that, if she could convey honor and respect for John with his current behavior, the *relationship* couldn't help but change because he would respond instinctively to her respect.

The bottom line is that Melanie's desire to change John had the effect of disempowering her. No one can force another person to change; that person will change only if he or she wants to change. Melanie had put all of her energy and frustration where it could not serve her. Through coaching, Melanie eventually recognized that the change she thought she needed from her boss was more about her own needs, not his. This doesn't mean that we shouldn't try to influence, inspire or motivate others. Quite the contrary, as discussed in Chapter 1—influence is a fundamental role of leadership. By looking at ourselves, we can influence, inspire and motivate others more successfully. Heart-centered leadership means acknowledging that, like Moses, we are human. It means having compassion for ourselves and others. It means honoring our humanness. It requires humbleness and showing humility. As Melanie was able to do this—to let go of her desire to change John—she experienced less stress and was more relaxed in her manner toward him.

Soliciting Feedback: Get Others to Help You Look in the Mirror

Those who are willing to do some soul-searching and take responsibility for their actions, thereby showing humility, often gain tremendous respect and valuable self-knowledge from their associates. We suggest that you conduct a 360-degree feedback process in two steps, (1) assessment and (2) reporting. This is one way of getting feedback from the people around you, according to the level of readiness of the organization. It may be helpful to conduct this process with a coach, who can help you debrief difficult feelings (e.g., fear, anxiety and self-recrimination).

First, using the list of heart-centered leadership characteristics on page 52, have your boss, peers and associates score you on these critical leadership characteristics. Feedback may be difficult to hear and to accept, but it is extraordinarily helpful in breaking the cycle of complaints, feelings of victimization and assignment of blame to others—common problems in organizations of all sizes. Receiving this feedback helps to bring the focus back where it belongs—on you.

Second, report feedback results to all participants as an acknowledgment of your willingness to change, vulnerability and "humanness." This renders you defenseless while gaining even more respect from those who completed your assessment. Why? Because it demonstrates your openness to constructive feedback from associates. In addition, because people know how difficult it is to look in the mirror, you gain your associates' respect by admitting developmental needs, because they realize how difficult this would be to do themselves.

After the second part of this process, it is common to hear that associates could not believe you stood before them and publicly admitted your faults. The common sentiment is that this takes incredible courage, and they are not sure they could have done this themselves. Talk about being a positive role model for your associates! When they see a leader's willingness to be humble, they are humbled as well. Being effective at leading ourselves opens us up to allow others to lead themselves.

Dan Ellinor, a regional president of Compass Bank, provides a good example of how this works. He expressed the importance of looking in the mirror and providing a process that would encourage his associates to do the same. In Dan's words:

> When I first arrived, I spent two weeks holding various small group meetings in order to meet with most of our employees and identify strengths that we should exploit, and weaknesses we should address. These groups were of about twenty employees. The foundation for these meetings was to find out three basic things— what works, what is not working, and what's next. Open communication is very important, and it needed to come from the very top. We also implemented a 360-degree feedback process for the leadership team. Each manager gets feedback from the entire leadership team, four peers and three direct reports, so a person could have up to nineteen responses. I was the first target to get the feedback. The good news is that fourteen months later this process is thriving.

Heart-Centered Leadership Characteristics

Look at the list below. Rate yourself from 1 to 10. A rating of 1 means you rarely display that particular characteristic; 10 means that you often display that characteristic.

		1	2	3	4	5	6	7	8	9	10
Attention	Pays careful attention in all situations										
Being Present	Is fully present and available at work and with others										
Compassion	Shows genuine care and concern for others										
Connections	Good at networking and brings people together										
Enthusiasm	Displays enthusiasm and spirit easily										
Gratitude	Expresses thanks and gratitude genuinely										
Hospitality	Makes others feel comfortable and puts them at ease										
Imagination	Creative; able to think outside the box; likes new ideas										
Joy	Good sense of humor; likes to celebrate; laughs easily										
Justice	Fair-minded; recognizes the equality and dignity of all										
Kindness	Has a kind and caring manner										
Listening	Listens well to others before speaking										
Meaning	Makes work meaningful for self and others										
Nurturing	Self-care; respects others' needs for self-care; avoids burnout										
Openness	Seen as approachable by all; easy to talk with										
Peace	Works well with conflict; able to mediate solutions										
Play	Playful; takes time to experiment; down to earth										
Reverence	Shows respect for spiritual forces that may be at work										
Shadow	Owns own defects and dark side; has nothing to hide										
Silence	Takes time out for reflection										
Teachers	Consults with own teachers, mentors, or advisors										
Transformation	Is willing to keep learning and changing										
Unity	Accepting of others and their roles; able to work harmoniously with a team										
Vision	Has a clear sense of vision; lives mission daily										

Figure 2.1

This list is adapted from the Alphabet of Spiritual Literacy developed by Frederic and Mary Ann Brussat in their books Spiritual Literacy[1] and Spiritual Rx.[2] For definitions and resources on these spiritual practices, see the Web site www.SpiritualityHealth.com. We recommend reviewing this site for information on characteristics for which you give yourself a lower rating.

How Do I Begin to "Know Thyself"?

There are many ways to know yourself, perhaps as many different ways as there are individuals. We don't suggest any one way as better than another, but we strongly recommend that you practice some formal method of self-reflection. We offer the following thoughts and ideas as a starting place. Take what you need and leave the rest. Remember, this list is for *you*, not for "them" or your boss or anyone else you would like to change. Also, recall Antoinette Samuel, quoted earlier in this chapter. The ultimate purpose in knowing yourself is as much for self-growth as for the growth of those you serve and work with every day. By knowing yourself, you have a better chance of helping your associates make a contribution.

1. **Shift your focus:** First and foremost, shift your mind-set to one of taking full and complete responsibility for whatever is happening in your life. Repeat this affirmation: *The world is what I make it. I am 100 percent responsible for my attitude.*

2. **Ask for feedback:** Knowing ourselves requires us to come to terms with our own strengths and development needs. How do you do that? Ask for feedback from all those who know you best. This does not have to be a formal 360-degree feedback process. When we work with a client and assist him or her in getting the proper feedback to begin this journey of self-knowledge, we have a conversation with the key individuals who know him or her best, even including the client's significant other. Ask for feedback, and be appreciative of all that you receive. Recognize that you may be inclined to disagree or explain some of this feedback; know that people's perceptions count, whether you agree with them or not. Something caused these individuals to formulate their impression of you. Take a serious look at this feedback, and do what you can to own it.

3. **Self-reflection:** Block out time to review and appraise yourself—daily or weekly. After reviewing all of the events, phone calls,

e-mails, meetings, conversations, etc., that occurred that day or week, ask yourself the following questions:

- What did I do to contribute to or take away from the success of these events?
- What mistakes did I make?
- On a scale of 1 to 10 (10 being highest), what number did I earn this day or week in terms of leading in a heart-centered way?
- What could I do to move higher on the scale?

4. **Keep track of destructive and constructive internal dialogue**: Keeping track of thoughts that serve you and don't serve you is useful. What kind of messages are you sending yourself? Recording those thoughts can be most useful in recognizing patterns of thinking. For example, consider the case of Paul:

Paul had a message that often ran through his mind about his associates. Basically, the message was that his associates were stupid. Paul—through coaching—eventually realized that his associates sensed his judgmental and negative thinking. Because they knew that he thought they were stupid, his associates had a natural and immediate dislike and distrust for Paul. Needless to say, Paul wasn't able to get much accomplished through his team. The associates began to do more stupid things, further reinforcing Paul's feelings about them. But where did this all begin, with the associates or with Paul? Was it really possible that all of his highly paid, respected associates were stupid?

Paul went through a self-discovery task that allowed him to identify and record every time he thought that "an associate (Jack, Fred, Mary) was stupid." He simply wrote on a piece of paper in his pocket what event triggered the thought—the situation and his emotional response to it. Once he took time to identify these events, he was able to analyze what happened and, more important, was able to identify a pattern in his thinking. After Paul reflected on this, he understood that he felt insecure and stupid. To protect himself from that thought, he projected it onto others.

Once Paul came to terms with this, he successfully shifted his thinking and filled his head with more-positive thoughts. Paul was willing to know himself more fully; he wanted to look in the mirror and take personal responsibility for all that happened to him and his team. He explored how his thinking not only didn't serve him personally; it also didn't serve his team—and, in the long term, it didn't serve Paul professionally. By Paul's willingness to "know thyself" and become a better self-leader, he showed more empathy for others who, he realized, had the same human struggles as he. In turn, he served as a role model for his associates.

It is important to note that while in this scenario, Paul's feeling of inadequacy projected into the thoughts he had of his team (they were stupid). We may make unwise hiring decisions and, in fact, end up with associates who are less than bright. Even if this is the case, we must take personal responsibility for the hiring decision, and ask ourselves how we can learn to hire the best possible associates.

To know thyself takes a great deal of courage. We are continually in awe not only of clients willing to do so, but also the tremendous impact that doing so has on their lives. If we don't take the time to look in the mirror and see ourselves, we can be blindsided.

5. **Continuing education**: Another way to "know thyself" is through experiential and educational avenues. There are numerous books and courses available to help: explore and understand yourself as a leader, identify your fears and concerns about working with others in a leadership position, and release your fears about increasing your vulnerability as a heart-centered leader. Because we see heart-centered leadership as a spiritual journey of self-knowledge, we also recommend that you pursue a course of continuing spiritual education.

6. **Therapy, counseling and coaching**: Sometimes professional counseling or psychotherapy is necessary to help uncover the blocks to leadership that we discussed in the introduction to this book. Too often, people in positions of power and leadership believe that

participating in a program of counseling or therapy is a sign of weakness or problems. Even today, knowing that counseling can be helpful in solving problems, people still stigmatize mental health concerns. In fact, it is often beneficial to seek counseling, and we recommend many different avenues through which you can find the right type of counselor or coach for you. You can seek out a pastoral counselor (for a list, visit the Web site of the American Association of Pastoral Counselors at www.aapc.org). Pastoral counseling can help you weave together your spiritual inclinations with your own psychological concerns about being a better leader. There is also a variety of certified mental health counselors and therapists in your state. You can find these through such associations as the American Mental Health Counselors Association (www.amhca.org, or call 800-964-2000). If your company has an Employee Assistance Program (EAP), you may be able to access a counselor immediately through a confidential number. To find an EAP provider near you, visit www.eapassn.org/public/providers. Alternatively, you can find a coach who is skilled in working with difficult blocks. Visit the coach referral Web site at www.coachreferral.com. Finally, we think that some blocks cannot be fully addressed through verbal or psychological work, and you may need to do some physical work by finding the right massage therapist, chiropractor or other form of alternative healing. These forms include neurolinguistic programming or holographic repatterning (www.holographic.org).

Examples of Spiritual Practices

The chart below is adapted from the list of "prescriptions" in Spiritual Rx: Prescriptions for Living a Meaningful Life *by Frederic and Mary Ann Brussat and is used with the authors' permission. To see the full list of practices for enhancing self-knowledge, visit the Web site, www.SpiritualityHealth.com.*

Practice	Enhances	Balances/Counters
Attention	Awareness	Distraction, stress
Being present	Contentment	Living in past or future
Compassion	Caring	Judgment, pain
Connections	Holistic way of life	Separations, dualisms
Enthusiasm	Energy	Apathy, boredom
Gratitude	Satisfaction	Greed, entitlement
Hospitality	Tolerance	Hostility, criticalness
Imagination	Creativity	Rationalism
Joy	Happiness	Sadness, sorrow
Justice	Equality, dignity	Oppression, fanaticism
Kindness	Generosity	Selfishness
Listening	Discernment	Disregard for others
Love	Intimacy	Fear
Meaning	Understanding	Cynicism, shallowness
Nurturing	Balance	Deprivation, codependency
Openness	Empathy, flexibility	Close-mindedness
Peace	Serenity, equanimity	Anger, violence, worry
Play	Free-spiritedness	Earnestness, predictability
Reverence	Worth, awe	Wastefulness, ennui
Shadow	Wholeness	Pollyannaism, projections
Silence	Contemplation	Chaos
Teachers	Wisdom	Pride
Transformation	Healing, growth	Resistance to change
Unity	Harmony, solidarity	Loneliness, individualism
Vision	Idealism	Pragmatism
Zeal	Passionate life	Unlived life

Figure 2.2

Exercise for "Knowing Thyself"

Heart-centered leaders are willing to look at their own characteristics—just as Moses did, as described earlier in this chapter, or the people who are willing to look at "the logs in their own eyes" before commenting on the specks in their neighbors. Take a look at the list of characteristics on page 52 and reflect on whether they describe you. Make a copy of the page and give it to those people in your life who you think know you well, as well as to a few associates with whom you work. Be aware that there are no right or wrong answers. Rather, discern which qualities (1) need further development and (2) are "blind spots"—that is, you rated yourself high on them while others rated you low. We recommend going to www.spiritualityhealth.com and doing the practices associated with those qualities requiring some work. Be patient with and easy on yourself.

Chapter 3
Don't Judge, Don't Assume; Come to Understand
(Your Open-Mindedness)

Do not judge, and you will not be judged; do not condemn, and you will not be
condemned. Forgive, and you will be forgiven; give, and it will be given to you.
For the measure you give will be the measure you get back.
—*Luke* 6: 37–38 *(abbreviated) RSV*

Do you think that an associate wakes up in the morning, jumps out of bed, and says, "I think I will mess up today; I think I will disappoint everyone around me today." We don't believe that human beings do this. And yet our associates make mistakes every day, just like we do. The vast majority of people have positive intentions, even though their behavior doesn't always reflect this. Imagine how differently you will communicate with an associate if you are grounded in this principle: People have positive intentions. Everything will shift. Instead of immediately judging the associate for the inappropriate behavior, you will begin by being more empathetic toward him or her. As a result, you will have a greater understanding of the causes of inappropriate behavior and gain more insight into the best solution.

We believe it is possible to develop your empathic ability. It requires correcting certain habits of mind, like taking sides in a conflict, and replacing them with healthier habits, like taking the perspective of both sides. It requires taking responsibility for your own habits of thinking, such as stereotypes, snap judgments and certain prejudices about what people "should" do.

Taking Sides
We received a call from a department head of a large, private university. The department chair explained that members of his department were

unable to work together as a team, and the conflict was beginning to affect the students. Further investigation revealed that two individuals—Bob and Fred—did not get along, and the rest of the department was taking sides. The department was divided into two camps. The associates involved had worked together for several years, and some had years of built-up conflict. We were called in to conduct a team-building session, but we knew that no progress could be made with the collective team until the individuals at odds with one another resolved their differences.

Bob and Fred were willing to meet with us so we could provide mediation services—a process that requires an individual to communicate the "how, what and why" of his or her feelings toward the other person. As is typical in these situations, Bob and Fred communicated a great deal of misunderstandings, assumptions and incorrect information about each other.

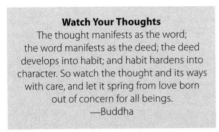

Watch Your Thoughts
The thought manifests as the word; the word manifests as the deed; the deed develops into habit; and habit hardens into character. So watch the thought and its ways with care, and let it spring from love born out of concern for all beings.
—Buddha

In fact, as the meeting progressed, they were amazed to discover they had much in common and actually admired each other in some ways. Bob and Fred left the session agreeing to work together as much as possible. They agreed to disagree on some items, and both admitted that each would have to rebuild trust in the other, which would take some time.

Are things between Bob and Fred perfect today? No. Are things better? Yes. Before the mediation session, both parties judged and made incorrect assumptions about each other. They both held on (or were attached) to their judgments and assumptions. Until the mediation session, they made no attempt to reach an understanding. Judgments, assumptions and the unwillingness to understand one another affect us all, both personally and professionally. In this case, these two individuals actually contributed to the creation of a stressful environment. Years of conflict affected the morale and productivity of the whole team and the students they were there to serve. The stress accumulated because Bob and Fred were unable to communicate without judging, or were assuming the worst in the other.

Two important lessons can be learned from this example. The first has to do with projection, or blame, and the importance of being aware of our own thoughts. We often project onto others what is mostly hidden in our thoughts. When we judge harshly and assume the worst, this is expressed verbally and nonverbally. Our words and our actions then create impressions that can gain strength over time. The power of thought is so great that Bob was able to convince one half of the department that Fred was the problem, while Fred persuaded the other half to take his side. So watch your thoughts! Refrain from *assuming* that you have to take sides or *judge* that someone is right and the other is wrong. Instead, *come to understand* players on both sides of the fence.

The second lesson of this story involves seeking help and getting a mediator involved. Fortunately, the department head was willing to get outside help, but Bob and Fred also had to be willing to come to the table. Sometimes, try as we might to lead in a heart-centered way, certain conflicts and long-term animosities can prevail. In these situations, we strongly encourage outside help. The professional practice of conflict mediation has grown significantly in the past few years, and it is not difficult to find someone to help. The department head could have continued to shrug off the problem and say with despair: "Some people just don't get along, and there is nothing I can do!" So, like him, we encourage you to get help, and *don't assume* that conflict is always a problem—get someone to help both sides *understand* each other.

Developing Perspective

There have been a growing number of reports of airline passengers acting abusively toward airline personnel. The number of incidents reported by all airlines attributable to "air rage" rose from 296 in 1994 to 921 in 1997.[1] These incidents of air rage are significant enough to warrant new legislation to help prevent problems and prosecute violators. Unfortunately, we continue to see more examples of judging and assuming, and less understanding beween the traveling public and airline personnel. What causes air rage?

On the surface, it seems that some passengers are just irrational by nature; they're irritable, hostile, bad-tempered or uncontrollable. Sometimes this judgment reflects the truth—some passengers who "flip out" have a history of mental problems. More often, however, air rage is not due to mental disorder. It is human nature to place blame on an individual, something psychologists call the "fundamental attribution error." This means that—as perceivers of others—we often attribute the cause of a person's behavior to personality or basic character rather than to the surrounding situation. The

> **Road Rage**
> Think about this the next time you are in traffic, someone cuts in front of you or otherwise acts in a hostile way. Take a breath and ask yourself... "I wonder what difficulties that man is facing in his life? Too bad. I hope he has a better day." Thinking this way will save you a lot of misery.

facts suggest that the causes of air rage often are more complex and situational. If we look below the surface, factors contributing to air rage may include: passenger alcohol use, a stressful flight environment, overbooking and increased passenger loads, other stressors involved in a particular flight, passengers' inability to control the cabin environment, toxins, oxygen depletion in the cabin and other factors.

As we see it, much air rage can be averted through empathy and understanding on both sides, passengers and airline personnel alike. What has happened to our compassion? Many flight attendants work a grueling schedule and live in the cramped space of airplanes for hours each day. Can we be a little more understanding of the stress they face? What about the passenger who has been treated coldly by airline personnel? What about the poor parent with a screaming child? Why do we look at this parent with expressions of hate and disgust when he or she is doing everything possible to calm the child? Do we not have any understanding for the parent's predicament?

We think that air rage—perhaps an extreme example—illustrates to the heart-centered leader the importance of taking the other's perspective. Perhaps the next time an associate does something that we did not request, we can pause long enough to say to ourselves, "Perhaps Gerry has positive intentions; I won't assume that my associate chose to mess up this project. I need to talk to Gerry about this project so I can better understand this behavior." If you approach Gerry with this thought, rather than the thought, "Gerry is stupid (or careless or purposely letting us down)," what might be the result? We predict you will gain a tremendous amount of information to help you understand Gerry's approach to the project. From there, you are better emotionally prepared to coach Gerry for success. What is the probable outcome? A better relationship with Gerry, a more highly motivated associate, and a greater likelihood of completing the project correctly. Punishing or judging someone rarely yields a positive outcome. It lowers the self-esteem of the associate and damages the relationship between the two of you, and the project may never be successfully accomplished.

Hiding Our Thoughts (A Tale of Close-Mindedness)

The importance of "coming to understand" is illustrated by an executive named Carol, who was derailing her career. Carol's lack of interpersonal skills affected the productivity of the team. Morale was low; in fact, her department's turnover was the highest in the company. Other issues screamed out that a problem needed fixing. Carol spent her first hour of coaching complaining about the incompetence of her team: "People just don't want to work anymore today. You just can't find good help anymore. My boss just doesn't realize what it is like to work with such a class of people." She made a great many assumptions and judgments regarding her team members. She was closed-minded. Making no attempt to understand the behavior of the team or why there was much turnover and low morale, Carol assumed it was because they were not educated or high-class people.

As Carol talked, it became clear that she grossly underestimated her own impact on the team. Carol could not see that the "buck stops here"—that, as a leader, she had some personal responsibility for the actions and outcomes of her team. Again, instead of trying to understand their behavior, she judged her associates and became angry with them, fueling a war among her and her team. A war which, by the way, the team was winning! How was the team winning? Two very senior, well-respected associates walked out on the job, saying they would not tolerate Carol's behavior any longer.

Self-Assess Your Open-Mindedness

Rate yourself on the following items, using the scale below.

Strongly Disagree	Disagree	In Between	Agree	Strongly Agree
1	2	3	4	5

1. I am tolerant of other people's lifestyles and am a broad-minded person.	
2. People who know me would not consider me "set in my ways."	
3. I am not quick to judge people.	
4. I find it easy to feel what others are feeling.	
5. I think it is a good thing to always be open to new ideas and perspectives.	
6. I am comfortable talking with others from different backgrounds or political persuasions.	

To assess your attitude of open-mindedness, total your scores for the above six items. Your score should range from a low of 6 to a high of 30.

10 or below – Much more closed-minded than open-minded
11 to 16 – Relatively closed-minded
17 to 20 – Some open-mindedness
21 to 25 – Relatively open-minded
26 to 30 – Highly open-minded

That got the attention of upper management, who insisted that Carol get coaching. Carol was so angry with her team and her boss for forcing her to get coaching that she spent most of the first few sessions blaming everyone but herself. She had a difficult time owning any part of what was happening with her team, even though she was the leader.

Through coaching, Carol eventually was able to take personal responsibility for her actions, and she actually sought guidance on what else she could do so that she would not slide back to her old way of thinking. How was she able to make such a turnaround? She finally looked in the mirror and took responsibility for her portion of the problem. Eventually, she allowed herself to show some vulnerability and humility. Once this happened, everything shifted—meaning that her thoughts and behavior changed with relation to her team.

One of the most intriguing things about human behavior is that many of us believe we can hide our thoughts from others. We cannot hide anything! In fact, this is the paradox of being close-minded versus open-minded: we think our associates don't know how we feel and/or think about them. They sense it all! Human beings are incredibly intuitive, and we have a great capacity to sense how someone feels about us. Carol was blind to the fact that thoughts she had about her associates—being lazy, not wanting to work, not educated—were coming across loud and clear. In fact, when interviewing her associates during the 360-degree feedback process, many said they knew of Carol's feelings toward them. Carol was shocked to discover the accuracy of their perceptions—she had never disclosed her judgments. Of course, they sensed it from her because it was the truth, and, again, as human beings, we are designed to sense the truth.

The bottom line here is to be more open-minded, which means it is not our role to be the judge, jury and executioner. Who among us has not made a mistake? When we make a mistake, don't we know it? So how does it serve for someone to tell us we made a mistake? What good will that do in the long run? Will it bring us satisfaction, and for how long? More times than not, we jump to a conclusion or misread an action for which we want to dole out punishment. For what purpose? The more we judge others, the more we will be judged. The more we condemn others, the more we will be condemned. Why? Because that is the type of energy that we generate. That is our focus, and, therefore, that is what will come back.

> Never judge people, don't type them too quickly, but in a pinch, always assume that a man is good and that at worst he is in the gray area between good and bad.
> —Gordon Dean, former head of the Atomic Energy Commission; scrawled on the back of an envelope found beside him after his death in a plane crash[2]

Overwhelmed

Sue found herself in a new job that was completely overwhelming. She worked in one city and lived in another. She experienced tremendous stress, worked long hours and spent less time with her family. When she did return home, she was upset with her husband for having not cleaned the house the way she felt it should be cleaned (her husband was a stay-at-home dad who took care of the kids). Needless to say, Sue wasn't very pleasant when she was at home. And she became so overwrought that she experienced a stress attack and ended up in the hospital. In a coaching session, Sue explored how she could improve the situation.

> *Coach:* Are you in a financial position to hire a cleaning service?
> *Sue:* Sure.
> *Coach:* Would your husband support the idea of having a house cleaner?
> *Sue:* Yes.
> *Coach:* Based on your schedule and your limited time at home, would you consider having a house cleaner clean on the day that you return home, every Friday?
> *Sue:* Well, my husband should clean the house! That is part of his job as a stay-at-home dad.
> *Coach:* Well, is the house getting clean?
> *Sue:* No.

Coach: What benefit is there in thinking that your husband should be cleaning the house when, in fact, it isn't being done?
Sue: When you put it that way, I guess there is no real benefit.
Coach: What cost is there in thinking that your husband should be cleaning the house when it is not being cleaned?

Sue realized there was a high cost. Her relationship with her husband had suffered, and her anger and frustration were taken out on the kids as well. She realized that she could continue to judge her husband for not doing what she assumed he should do. *Judging* him, of course, was *not* getting the house clean. In fact, her judgment was not only *not* getting the house clean, but was also creating additional problems for her. Sue saw that she was putting all of her energy in the wrong place, so she hired a house cleaner to come once a week to coincide with the day that she returned home.

We spend too much time focusing on what we think someone should, would and could be doing. We think we are going to change someone, or we waste a great deal of time and energy trying. It has been proven over and over that telling someone to change will not create change—change happens only when a person wants to change. However, when we change ourselves, everything else shifts. In Sue's case, the reality was that her expectations (and resulting judgment, anger and irritability) were not resolving the issue, and her desire to change her husband was not getting the house clean. Sue also knew that she and her husband needed to agree on the division of household responsibilities and determine the root cause of her husband's inability to clean the house.

Effort and Shifting the Situation

It takes some effort, but when you become open-minded—not assuming and not judging—and you understand the other's point of view, everything shifts for you as well as for your associates. Your whole approach toward the person changes; you become much more compassionate, and that is sensed by the other person. Imagine how much more you can get accomplished when you make every effort to understand the behavior of your associates rather than automatically assuming you know what happened or what they are thinking.

We are either ruled by our thoughts, or we can make an effort to monitor and rule them. How we choose to think about others is determined by many factors; only one of these factors is our experience of the other person. Other important factors that determine our ability to empathize—to come to understand—include intelligence, our willingness to take responsibility, and a more open-minded, flexible or less simplistic (black-and-white) view of the world. Most important, as a heart-centered leader, is your own *willingness to pause* before rushing to judgment, and to *make an effort* to consider alternative viewpoints. As in the stories shared above, you can ask yourself— as did Bob and Fred, Carol, and Sue—"What does it benefit me to judge the other or to think he or she sees the world the way I do?"

All of the noise in our heads keeps us from heart-centered leadership. Think about it. How can any person have the exact experiences in life as you? Therefore, it doesn't make sense that our thoughts would be the same. What we think is the obvious answer may not be the answer to another. When we *come to understand*, we will unveil all the barriers that separate us from others. No two people are going to experience a given reality in the same way. When you lose your need to be right, when you stop judging, interpreting, assuming, labeling or analyzing, there will be silence in your mind. If we practice this new way of thinking, our relationships have a greater chance to become open, loving and heartfelt.

There is an old sage's story about a man who was steering his canoe through a dark fog on the lake one morning. The man could not see very far in front of him, but was able to discern some objects from each other. All of a sudden, he saw the shape of a boat, a small dinghy, that was headed directly for him. He thought that the person in that boat also could not see him. He immediately started waving his arms around wildly and shouted: "Stop! You are headed right for me! Watch out!" In his frantic haste, the man tipped over his own canoe and landed in the water. He held on to his canoe and started screaming at the passing boat: "Who do you think you are? You complete idiot. You..." As suddenly as he saw the boat coming, the man—now all wet and upset—realized that there was no one at all in the passing dinghy. It had apparently come loose from its moorings, and was drifting aimlessly in the lake.

There are many things to learn from this story. We have a very strong tendency to blame, get defensive and think that someone or some force is behind the stresses that come our way. We make the fundamental attribution error and "read" personality or character into the actors who make mistakes in our lives. But if, instead of *assuming or judging*, we take a moment to relax and gain perspective, we might see that most of the time there is really nothing to react to. Our own thoughts and reactions account for most of the problems we face. The world is what we make it. So, how could the man steering the canoe behave differently? Could he have simply and quietly stuck his oar out in front of him and gently guided his own canoe around the empty dinghy?

> He who knows nothing is closer to the truth than he whose mind is filled with falsehoods and errors.
> —Thomas Jefferson

Introduction to the Exercise

In earlier chapters, we stressed the importance of three abilities: (1) listening for the human element, (2) distinguishing management from heart-centered leadership and (3) looking at yourself in the mirror. The stories in this chapter reflect four different but related tendencies that can hamper your ability to take the next step and really *practice* heart-centered leadership. The crucial next step is to *exhibit* behaviors that indicate to others that you sincerely seek to understand them. Four blocks are discussed in this chapter:

1. **Resentments**: Jumping to conclusions, taking sides, holding grudges and resentments, and staying attached to our judgments of others. These were at the root of the conflict between Bob and Fred.
2. **Lack of Perspective**: Failing to view the particular set of stresses or situations from another's perspective. This was discussed as a significant factor underlying air rage.
3. **Complaining**: Complaining or condemning others, or harshly judging their character based on appearance, education level or your own standards. Complaining first (and asking questions later) was the problem Carol faced with her work team.
4. **Lack of Support/Coping Ability**: Failing to consider your own stress levels, work overload, poor or maladaptive coping abilities, lack of self-care or impact of major life changes. Sue's new job put an extra burden on her, affecting her ability to think clearly about the cost and benefits of hiring a house cleaner. She was externally focused versus taking care of herself first.

Each of these four blocks has an opposite or an antidote, as shown in the figure below.

Blocks to Understanding	Antidote	Affirmative Thought
Resentments	Serenity	I forgive. May I be free of anger and resentment. I show the same tolerance and patience toward others that I would expect.
Lack of Perspective	Empathy	How can I help? I seek to understand the world from another's perspective.
Complaining	Praising	I support others in their growth. I say and do positive things to help them.
Lack of Support/ Coping Ability	Relaxation	I adjust well to stress, balancing work and home activities with care for self and others. Note: Chapter 8 on Principle Seven—Care for the Heart—is devoted to dealing with this block.

Figure 3.1

Exercise

To begin this exercise, pick any one of the four blocks with which you have a problem. Your assignment is to consciously note any time you have a thought in the category you chose. Ideally, it helps to set aside one day during the work week for this exercise, keeping your journal with you so you can record your thoughts as they occur. You can also simply keep a tally of each time you have a thought in one of the four areas. Do this exercise for at least one full day. On the second day, record your thoughts, but practice replacing each negative thought with the appropriate positive affirmation.

There are three objectives of this exercise: (1) to train your mind to observe itself, (2) to identify blocks to understanding and (3) to retrain your mind to hold positive thoughts that help understanding. To get you started in identifying which block you want to work on, here are some examples of the kinds of thoughts you might have:

Resentments	Name calling; "if only he or she ..."; "Why do I always have to be the one who ...?"; "I simply cannot accept ..."; "I'll show them"
Lack of Perspective	"He is just looking out for himself"; "Incompetent"; "Loafer"; "Why can't people ...?"; "It's his or her fault that..."
Complaints	Any negative judgment or criticism; whining; accusing; vindictiveness; sarcasm; lamenting; scowling; snapping; rolling your eyes; grumbling; sniveling
Lack of Support/ Coping	"I don't trust him or her to get the job done"; "My co-workers are unfriendly"; "People here just don't get along"

Figure 3.2

Chapter 4
They Need What You Need (Authenticity)

Do unto others as you would have them do to you.
—Luke 6:31 RSV

Do the right thing. It will gratify some people and astonish the rest.
—Mark Twain

What does this title—"They Need What You Need"—mean? The simple truth
is that your associates are human beings just like you. In the busy, sometimes
jaded and alienating business world, it may seem trite to think that we are one
and the same. However, your needs—either to accomplish something, to be
valued, told the truth, appreciated, loved, wanted, cared for and about, to make
a difference or make a positive contribution to others—overlap to a great extent
with your associates' needs. We forget that our associates want nothing more
or less than we do. We are all shareholders in basic human and interpersonal
needs. To a great extent, we share the common needs to accomplish, serve,
and be the reason for someone else's happiness and well-being.

We conducted a survey of nearly 1,000 associates within a hospitality/
hotel service organization, asking them to rank six different career goals in
relative importance. We also identified whether an associate, supervisor or
general manager answered the survey. We found that associates put their first
career goal in one of two categories: they either wanted to "accomplish
something, master a skill or become an expert at my job," or they wanted to
"make an important contribution or know that I was of service to others."
Chart 4.1 on the next page shows the percentage of survey respondents who
ranked these and other goals as their most important. As the chart shows,
23 to 32 percent of all associates—regardless of position—ranked the desire
to accomplish or master their job as the most important goal. Also, 17 to 25
percent ranked the desire to make a contribution as most important.

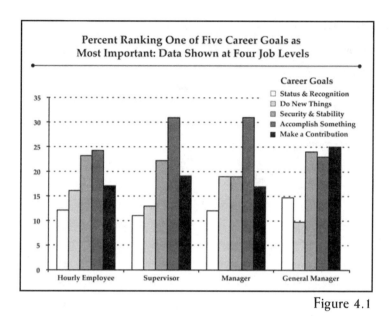

Percent Ranking One of Five Career Goals as Most Important: Data Shown at Four Job Levels

Career Goals
- ☐ Status & Recognition
- ☐ Do New Things
- ☐ Security & Stability
- ■ Accomplish Something
- ■ Make a Contribution

Figure 4.1

There were some distinguishing factors across job levels, but the similarities seemed to outweigh these differences. For example, general managers tended to rank "make a contribution" higher than others, and managers were more likely to want a career that gave them "new things to do, new roles and jobs to try." For the most part, however, goals such as status, recognition and security were less important than goals that involved making a contribution to or having some impact on others. Of real interest, the need for accomplishment appears to increase until one achieves the "general manager" position. At that point, accomplishment needs lessen, and the desire to make a lasting contribution reaches its peak.

These results suggest several things to us. First, if we are willing to look, we will find that our associates (supervisor or subordinate) often share personal career goals very similar to our own. The ability to understand this commonality, and to tap into it, is the key to not judging your associates. Second, as we move into positions of greater responsibility, the desire for social contribution and a care for the greater good become more important. This is another key to heart-centered leadership.

Thinking About What Others Need

If we follow our hearts, we do not need to be motivated to give our best effort by some external or prescribed management "trick of the month." If we listen, our hearts will tell us to think about what others need, and to consider their perspectives and how our own actions might affect them. If we listen, we often find that our associates want to hear the truth, be respected and be treated as authentic and productive partners. By now, you may be thinking, "This sounds great, but I have an associate who is clueless. He doesn't understand the job, and I have to deal with that behavior." We realize how difficult it can be to talk of heart-felt behavior when associates are

> There is no question that the motivation to work varies widely in people. Therefore, managers must be flexible in their leadership approach so they may be more participative with certain employees while taking a much more directive approach with others. Managers must try to create an environment and climate where employees can express their full potential and respond to difficult challenges by letting go of fear of failure, fear of change, or fear of risk taking.[1]

inefficient, when things seem to be falling apart all around you, and when it seems that we live in a dog-eat-dog world. We also realize that from a strict management perspective, the job has to get done yesterday! The question for leaders is *how* to motivate those associates we might otherwise judge as clueless, unproductive and lackluster.

We believe the answer lies in *how* we think about associates' needs or the position we take in motivating others. It may help to recall the distinctions among manager, leader and heart-centered leader (see Chapter 1). Managers tend to think about their associates' needs very differently than about leaders' needs. With management's emphasis on reason, control and organization, there is a tendency to view associates as needing direction, safety and security, rules, regulations and guidelines, as well as rewards in terms of a paycheck, a reasonable amount of time off and a vacation. Leaders, who by definition are focused on vision, creativity and building a team, tend to view associates as needing to develop themselves and to feel successful, to belong, participate and be recognized, and to exercise their minds, talents and creative spirits.

When practicing heart-centered leadership, you have more flexibility when thinking about "they need what you need." Sometimes you wear the manager's hat and recognize associates' needs for security and guidance. Sometimes you wear the leader's hat and recognize the need for creativity and belonging. However, in addition to and overriding these perspectives is your own willingness to be vulnerable and your ability to set aside yourself and your own needs in order to serve others—to make a difference and a positive contribution. In other words, heart-centered leadership requires paying attention to the particular or idiosyncratic needs and desires of any individual associate. You have a sense of the person as an individual and try to meet the person, wherever he or she is, whatever needs he or she may have. You lead by encouragement and inspiration, not by fear and control.

In making these distinctions, we are not suggesting a formula or prescription. Once again, it is important to talk about the control we think we have over others. In the long run, we are not going to change people through our efforts at control; we can only invite them to get on board with us. The focus should be on ourselves. It all starts with our thoughts and, most important, *how we think about others*, determining how we act toward them, which determines how they treat us. This is why it is so helpful to think about what others, as individual persons, truly need. It helps us understand the consequences of our actions—a very important trait of good leadership!

We think a theme from the previous chapter bears repeating: "Thoughts become words and words become action." Let's experiment with this notion a little further. In one of our leadership class exercises, we ask for three volunteers to participate in a role play. Two of them are given specific instructions on how to think about another person, the third volunteer. These two volunteers are given a script to read aloud, and are asked to take turns reading the script with the given thought in mind.

The only difference in their instructions is what the first two volunteers are told to think about the third volunteer as they read the script. Volunteer #1 is asked to think that he or she really likes the person and has great admiration and respect for him or her. Volunteer #2 is asked to think that he or she really dislikes the person and has little to no respect for him or her. The rest of the class is instructed to observe what they see. The class has no idea of the thoughts we asked the two volunteers to have as they read their script to the third partner.

In doing this exercise, 100 percent of the audience observed a distinct difference in the behavior and outcome of reading the script. All could see there appeared to be a good, positive relationship with one partner and a very negative relationship with the other. When we debriefed the exercise, participants were amazed at how much of the person's feelings about the other are projected in the way they treat the person. Since both volunteers were given exactly the same script to read, the difference wasn't the words. Instead, each person's thoughts projected from his or her tone of voice and body language toward the other. This entire behavior came from how they *thought about* their partner and his or her needs and motivations.

> This above all: to thine own self be true, and it must follow, as the night the day, thou canst not then be false to any man.
> —William Shakespeare

Authenticity and the Need for Truth

One lesson from this exercise is the importance of watching your thoughts, for they are truly projected, and the recipient is picking them up. The deeper lesson has to do with authenticity, with our inner truth, with revealing ourselves, and with our willingness to be vulnerable. Of all the different needs that we have, and that we share with our associates, one of the most important is the need to be told the truth; the need to be dealt with directly and authentically. We especially need to hear the truth from our leaders, those in whom we place our trust, and look to for guidance. We don't want to be betrayed and patronized, or "snake-oiled" and "sold a bill of goods."

Consider this from the perspective of a heart-centered leader. Nobody likes a liar. Your associates will be more likely to respect you if you tell the truth. In fact, associates are more satisfied with their jobs, less likely to experience stress, show up at work more often and are more productive when they trust their supervisors and feel their supervisors understand them and take their own perspectives. However, the

job of an executive, or any person in a leadership role, is often complex. It is not always appropriate to reveal the whole truth of a situation to associates. Leaders have to make some tough decisions about how much to share. Heart-centered leaders must balance directness and tactfulness when speaking the truth to associates. Such leaders have the courage to say something rather than withhold information, or talk only in official, formal language or on a "need-to-know" basis.

A vivid example of this occurred in New York City after the terrorist attacks on September 11, 2001. Mayor Rudolph W. Giuliani was named "Person of the Year (2001)" by *Time* magazine. In the face of the attacks "he led by emotions, not just by words and actions," said *Time* managing editor Jim Kelly. The magazine's editors chose Giuliani for "having more faith in us than we had in ourselves, for being brave when required and rude where appropriate and tender without being trite, for not sleeping and not quitting and not shrinking from the pain all around him."

These words of praise are due, in part, to Giuliani's willingness to tell the truth about problems with rescue efforts at Ground Zero. He did not speak in formal, official tones; for example, he did not say, "We are not able to ascertain the number of losses at this time, and it is difficult to gauge a fair estimate without further investigation." He did not say, "We cannot confirm or deny specifics about the losses at the World Trade Center." He did not say, "I am not at liberty to discuss the losses, but it is a sad day, indeed." Instead, he was vulnerable. At first, Giuliani was hopeful that survivors would be found, but he later admitted that such recovery was unlikely. He shared whatever information he had, he shared his feelings, and he stayed present throughout the difficult, horrifying and uncertain process of recovery. He spoke directly to and for the needs of the people, even when it meant being "rude," rather than hiding behind politically correct language.[2]

A Model for Truth-Telling

Many of us sense when we are not being told the truth. However, scandals within large companies like Enron and WorldCom suggest that financial systems can be structured to hide the truth. As mentioned above, leaders (like Mayor Giuliani) with great responsibility often have to make difficult decisions about what and how much to reveal. For some leaders motivated by less than heart-centered principles, the decision to hide information is easy. Unfortunately, the decision about what to disclose is not always motivated by the purest of intentions. The first principle in *Heart-Centered Leadership* is to "know thyself" (Chapter 2), which also translates as being truthful to yourself and knowing your own motives. We return to the message of Chapter 2, the importance of looking inside, because "inner vision" is essential for authentic leadership. In seeking to understand "they need what you need," you first must clear up some personal barriers to telling the truth, either because some of your associates will recognize these barriers anyway, or because you will be hurting only yourself. We have created a model to guide your understanding of truth-telling, your decision about when and how to tell the truth and your barriers to truth-telling.

The model we present in Figures 4.2-4.4 is an adaptation of the Johari Window.[3] First, imagine that your world is made up of all the things you know about yourself. Now divide that world into halves with a boundary between them. The first half represents your "face" to the world—what you share (through words and actions); the second half represents what you hide (e.g., motives, desires and needs). Unless you are a sociopath, a pathological liar or someone who hides everything from

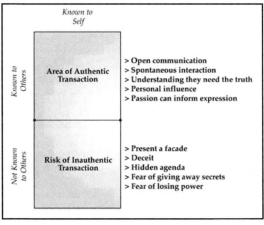

Figure 4.2

others, you are not likely to have a sharp boundary among your outer face and inner motives. In other words, as a human being, your words and actions often reflect inner motives and desires. Figure 4.2 shows the distinction between the two worlds of your known self. The area you know about and share with others we call "Authentic Transaction," characterized by open, spontaneous interaction. This is where you understand that "they need what you need." The area you hide from others is the area where you risk inauthentic transaction, present a facade, and often fear someone will discover secrets.

Now, imagine that there are parts of yourself of which you are unaware. This world is also divided into halves. One half is known to others and the other is not. Figure 4.3 shows the distinction between the two worlds of your unknown self. The part others see is called the "blind area" and contains your blind spots. The part that neither you nor others see represents either hidden potential or the dark side of leadership and organizational life.

It should be clear by now that your words and actions are not the only things your associates see or "read" about you. Your tone, vocal inflections, posture and other nonverbal behaviors come through loud and clear, especially when they don't match your words and actions. In other words, people pay attention to how you say things and how you act as much as, if not more than, what you say and do.

These diagrams provide a map for truth-telling. What we say and do is seemingly separate from our sometimes hidden needs and desires, and our needs and desires

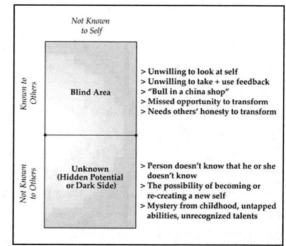

Figure 4.3

can be expressed in non-verbal ways. We may believe that people evaluate us only from our words and actions. What we actually show others, however, is more than words and actions, as suggested by the blind area in Figure 4.3. In short, the face we show the world is not always the face that our associates see.

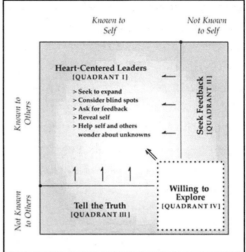

Figure 4.4

To use the map, heart-centered leaders have several tasks. First, they need to understand the four quadrants of the Johari Window and consider all the possibilities of inauthentic transaction, blind spots and unknown areas. They need to understand that their associates also have these four quadrants. Figure 4.4 shows the full map of all four quadrants.

Second, heart-centered leaders always seek to expand their area of "Authentic Transaction," or Quadrant I of the Johari Window. They do this in three ways: (1) telling the truth (disclosing) or moving information from Quadrant III to Quadrant I, (2) seeking honest feedback (asking) or moving information from Quadrant II to Quadrant I and (3) exploring and helping others explore hidden areas (transforming) or moving information from Quadrant IV to Quadrant I. Figure 4.4 shows the three tasks involved in expanding the area of authenticity.

There are many exercises you can do to fulfill these three tasks. These include open meetings, 360-degree feedback, one-on-one interviews, taking a personal inventory, working with a coach or holding a team retreat. We think the critical area underlying all these exercises is the ability to know your own motivations, how you express or hide them from your associates and how you consider the motivations of your associates. The exercise at the end of this chapter will help you with this.

Truth-Telling in the Organization: It Is Always a Decision

In their role of responsibility, leaders often deal with information and knowledge of their company or organization that is not in the public domain. That is, Quadrant III (where you can either tell the truth or risk inauthentic transaction) is part of many organizations because internal information is not readily available or observable by those outside the organization. This can be sensitive and important information about financial performance, liability concerns, political issues or the decreasing performance of a particular associate, department or division. Such information can be very important in determining the future actions you take with regard to the whole organization. You are faced with two decisions. First, you must decide how this information directs your actions. Second, you must decide how much, if any, of this information you withhold from or disclose to your associates. That is, you decide whether to move from Quadrant III to Quadrant I in Figure 4.4. Both of these decisions—what you decide to do and say in your words and actions—become part of the "face" you show the world. This "face" can be authentic (Quadrant I), or it can have blind spots, be inauthentic or simply have unknown qualities.

> **Some Definitions**
> - Authentic: original, first-hand, real, actual, genuine [as opposed to counterfeit, forged, etc.]
> - Authenticity: as being true in substance, as being genuine.
> - Genuine: natural, pertaining to the original stock, pure-bred, not spurious, being as represented, real, true, not counterfeit, unadulterated.
> - Author: the person who originates or gives existence to anything.

So there are two decision points we're describing. Decision Point 1 concerns how knowledge dictates action. How should you act, given what you "know" about the market, budget, performance, profits, timelines and customer needs? The key point we wish to emphasize concerns Decision Point 2 and, more important, how it is shaped by your own personal attitude of authenticity. In our experience, there are a number of factors that come into play. We list these here:

- You may think—in a managerial or military mode—that employees should get sensitive information only on a need-to-know basis. You may believe that it is best not to rock the boat with unnecessary information.
- You may believe that your associates can't handle the truth. This was the attitude depicted in the movie *A Few Good Men*, where Jack Nicholson played a Marine colonel who hid information in a court trial.
- You may believe that knowledge is power, and that if you give away important knowledge, you also give away your power.
- You may lack the ability to discern the difference between information that is important for associates to know and information that could be damaging. Because of this, you may be afraid of saying the wrong thing and hide behind official or politically correct language.
- You may enjoy a position of power because it gives you access to such sensitive and privileged information. This could lead you to feeling entitled to keep information because you believe it is meant only for "higher-ups" such as yourself.

We present this information for two reasons. First, we encourage you to examine your own level of authenticity and your attitude toward sharing information. Second, and more important, when you practice heart-centered leadership, it is critical to understand your associates' need for the truth, especially in uncertain situations (e.g., rapid change, shifting leadership, layoffs, downsizing and cultural change). There are also many situations where you have to make a judgment call, where divulging sensitive information can be damaging to the company or to certain parties. However, we believe there are many opportunities for courage, for thinking and acting differently and for showing true leadership. This is the risk of moving into Quadrant IV and exploring (with your associates) how to make better decisions in ways neither you nor they currently know.

One example of a company with a policy for truth-telling is The Container Store, a retail chain of stores headquartered in the Dallas, Texas, area. Among other things, the company is known to openly share its financials with associates. Based on data from 2001, the company's commitment to openness has helped maintain profitability and win numerous awards from *Fortune* magazine, *Workforce* magazine and the National Retail Federation.[4] Its truth-telling, along with other factors (e.g., commitment to training), has resulted in the firm's achievement of sustaining a 20 to 25 percent increase in annual sales each year. In addition, in an industry where 100 percent turnover is common, The Container Store boasts a very low 15 to 20 percent, and 41 percent of new hires come from employee referrals.

Would you consider doing this (obviously within the bounds of the law)? Why do companies hide this stuff anyway? Is it not true that associates are the first to hear or sense there are financial problems or successes anyway? What benefit could be derived from openly telling the truth to associates about where the company stands? How can we expect associates to rally for our organization's cause, and to help meet its goals and struggles, when they don't even have a clue as to what the goals and struggles are?

Shifting Perspective

A key factor in realizing these opportunities lies in shifting perspective—that is, walking a mile in the other's shoes. We have an incredible ability to perceive, to sense and to understand the real truth. Honesty and openness apply just as much to one-on-one relationships as they do in big-picture or group relationships. If the real truth is that you do not respect or like the person, that is what will be sensed. You simply cannot hide from the truth. If your thoughts about your associates are that they are strong, capable people, that is what will be projected. If, on the other hand, you have an associate with whom you are not pleased, that thought is projected as well. Imagine how different it could be if you consciously decide to think warm, respectful thoughts about an associate whom you have felt performs poorly? How will this person react to you? How will it differ from the past? If we make a conscious and distinct choice to approach an associate in a nonjudgmental and understanding manner, what will be the outcome? If we truly understand that we are all the same, how will our approach differ? And, in return, how will this person respond differently?

You will likely notice a shift in your associate's approach to you over time. Why? Because when we think loving, compassionate thoughts of others, we touch their hearts, and they become humbler in the process. They begin to break down the barriers of defense, because there is nothing against which to defend. Thus, there is some vulnerability in the meaning behind the phrase, "They need what you need."

Here is a story that helps convey this point of shifting perspective:

An aging farmer spends his time sitting idly because he has, over the years, gradually lost his ability to work in the fields and help grow and cultivate crops. His son—who has a family to feed and is still working the farm—looks at his father from time to time and judges him. "He's of no use anymore—he doesn't do anything!" One day the son becomes so frustrated that he builds a wooden coffin, drags it over to the porch and tells his father to get in. Without saying anything, the father climbs inside. After closing the lid, the son drags the coffin to the edge of the property where there is a high cliff. As the son approaches the drop, he hears a light tapping on the lid from inside the coffin. He opens it up. Still lying there peacefully, the father looks up at his son: "I know you are going to throw me over the cliff, but before you do, may I suggest something?" "What is it?" asks the son. "Throw me over the cliff, if you like," said the father, "but save this good wooden coffin. Your children might need to use it."[5]

Taking Our Own Inventory

We are reminded of a supervisor who expressed real frustration over how indifferently, and sometimes rudely, his employees treated him. This supervisor—we'll call him Alan—realized his contribution to the problem over the years and took responsibility for the impact he had on his associates. He also acknowledged that he could have done a lot of things differently, but that he'd supervised them the best way he'd known at the time. Here is how the conversation between Alan and his own manager, Tom, began:

Alan (supervisor), in a loud, complaining tone: I just wish these guys would treat me with more respect! I don't understand why they don't do things the way I want them done!

Tom (manager): Well, what do you mean by respect? Give me your definition of respect.

Alan, still upset: My key foreman will not contact me for days on end, unless I initiate the contact. He forgets meetings. It's just frustrating. I am out of the loop!

It was clear that Alan didn't understand that his foreman was modeling his behavior after Alan's own behavior toward others. The conversation continued:

Tom, in a comforting tone: It is really hard for you, and it may help to look at how you are with others, too.

Alan: What do you mean?

Tom: Well, all the frustration and behaviors you are talking about—feeling out of the loop and frustrated—is exactly what I have experienced from you. Many times, you forget to keep me up to date. There are many times I feel completely cut off from you, not hearing from you until after an important process is over—unless I initiate the call.

Alan, after a long pause and a sigh: Wow! I hadn't thought about that! You are right!

The feedback from Alan's manager was a complete revelation to him. You see, we don't really see ourselves. But how we treat others, how we respond to others, is what we get back from them. This goes back to the Golden Rule, "Do unto others as you would have them do unto you." Once Alan mentally pushed through this feedback, Tom helped him address his frustration about the foreman: *"Do you think that he senses how you feel about him?"* Alan had to admit that, yes, he probably did.

So, by shifting his thoughts toward the foreman, Alan can make a dramatic difference in the relationship. How do we do that? To shift our perspective to understand that "they need what you need" requires mentally viewing the person differently. As stated in previous chapters, this means coming from a place of understanding and *not* judgment, and *not* assuming the foreman is a louse. The relaxation of judgment requires us to be compassionate and to hold the thought: *This person is doing the best that he or she knows how to do.*

Ultimately, Alan shifted his approach toward the foreman by acknowledging that he himself had exhibited the same uncommunicative behavior. As a result, Alan and his foreman (and the rest of the crew) are performing more like a cohesive team. As in the story of the farmer son and his aging father, it requires acknowledging a basic shared vulnerability and the desire to treat others as we would like to be treated.

A Profound Understanding

The power of understanding this concept is profound. When we really understand our humanness and the fact that we are all connected, we understand that we all want the same things: to be respected, cared about, empathized with and listened to. So rather than looking outside yourself, start to ask yourself these basic questions:

- What am I doing to show respect for others?
- What am I doing to show care and concern for others?
- Am I illustrating to others what I want for myself?

And also hold the thought: *This person is doing the best that he or she knows how to do.* If you don't hold that thought, you will likely reap what you sow. The aim of treating people as we want to be treated is to honor others as inherently valuable, whole and complete, no matter how seemingly imperfect and unworthy they appear to us. As a leader, you can relate to those times in your career when a leader treated you disrespectfully or thought you were not qualified or deserving of a job or promotion or treated you as though you had no value. What was your response? You probably lost self-confidence, and, likely, your view of your own leader greatly suffered. So were you jumping for a chance to please this leader? Were you highly motivated to perform your best? We are sure you were not. Contrast this with a time when you worked for a leader who believed in you, cared about you and told you the truth. Do you recall how motivated you were to work for him or her? Probably very motivated. You want and need what your associates want and need—nothing more or less.

Exercise for Chapter 4

Step 1 (What You Need): Rank the six different types of career or job paths listed below on how important they are to you, using a scale from 1 to 6, with 1 being the most important to you. Make sure to use each of the numbers only once. There is no right or wrong answer to this exercise.

_____ *Do New Things*
I want my job /career to offer new things to do, new roles/jobs to try.

_____ *Accomplish Something*
I want to accomplish something, master a skill or become an expert at my job.

_____ *Have Security*
I want a stable career or a series of jobs within one organization.

_____ *Gain Status and Recognition*
I want my job to give me more status, a higher rank and recognition over time.

_____ *Make a Contribution*
I want to make an important contribution or know that I am of service to others.

_____ *Receive Money and Comfort*
I want fair compensation for my work, to earn enough money to live comfortably and to retire without financial worry.

Step 2 (Probing Further): After ranking these six needs or goals, look at your top two choices. Ask yourself if and how these top needs are expressed, and how they show up in your behavior as a manager or leader. In other words, do your associates see you how you see yourself? Consider the following: look at your top-ranked choice (Column A in Figure 4.5), and then ask yourself the questions in Columns B and C. It will help to write down your answers to these questions in your journal. You also may interview your associates to see whether your perceptions are accurate.

A) What You Ranked	B) Do Unto Others	C) Living Your Truth
If you ranked the following as 1 or 2, then:	…consider this for associates who have similar needs:	…consider this question:
Do New Things	Do your associates feel you provide a stimulating, challenging and interesting work environment?	How often does your current job allow you to try new things in ways that fulfill you?
Accomplish Something	Do your associates feel you help them to be successful and that they are accomplishing things?	How often does your current job allow you to accomplish things in ways that fulfill you?
Have Security	Do you help provide security and stability for those who desire it?	How often does your current job allow you to feel secure?
Gain Status and Recognition	Do your associates have fair and equal opportunity to achieve status and recognition when warranted?	How often does your job allow you to achieve the status and recognition you deserve?
Make a Contribution	Do your associates feel you help them make a contribution or be of service?	How often does your current job allow you to make a contribution or be of service?
Receive Money and Comfort	Do your associates know the financial status of the organization? Are they compensated fairly?	How often does your current job compensate you fairly and allow you to feel secure?

Figure 4.5

By answering the above questions, you should get some insight into how much you understand the needs of your associates (Column B) and also how much you are able to fulfill your needs (Column C). To be clear, the list of six needs is only a partial list, and may not accurately capture the most important needs for you. The point is that you start to look at how you think about "they need what you need," and how much you live your own truth.

Step 3 (Taking an Inventory): For a variety of reasons, we and our associates can't always follow our hopes and dreams; we can't always live out our needs. This is often due to a tight economy, changes at work, or any one of many stress factors that we face daily on the job. The point to ponder is *how we deal with it* when we cannot fulfill our needs or when we cannot help our associates to fulfill their needs.

For this next step, review the needs that you ranked as important and your answers in column C (Living Your Truth) in Figure 4.5. Then, using Figure 4.6, consider whether you have the feelings in the second column and/or whether you act out the feelings in the third column. Also, consider whether your associates may be acting a certain way because *they* experience barriers to meeting their own needs.

What You Ranked	If barriers exist, consider whether you...	
Top Ranked	… feel this way at work or your job	… act this way toward associates
Do New Things	Stagnant, bored, ineffective, in a "dead-end" job	Bureaucratic, micro-controlling, unmotivated
Accomplish Something	Apathetic, unconcerned	Unhelpful, insincere, unwilling to empower
Have Security	Victimized, used, manipulated	Manipulative, fearful
Gain Status and Recognition	Unimportant, alone, isolated	Distancing, unappreciative
Make a Contribution	Marginalized, like dead weight	Uncooperative, uncaring
Receive Money and Comfort	Devalued, cheapened	Disorganized, undirected

Figure 4.6

Look at how your own frustrated or thwarted needs lead to certain feelings or attitudes which, in turn, can affect your behavior toward others. If you are having difficulty in one of these areas, here are some positive affirmations or statements that may help you. The purpose of this exercise is positive: to make you aware of factors that keep you from considering the needs of others and to help you make more of an effort to consider such needs. Use the following positive affirmations for this purpose.

Positive Affirmations When Needs Are Thwarted
Do New Things
I work in a job or career that vitalizes me and is filled with pleasant surprises, always giving me new things to do, new roles and fulfilling tasks.

Accomplish Something
I accomplish something important every day, expressing my talents and mastering skills. I am an expert at my job.

Have Security
I am a loyal and dedicated leader who brings stability and security to those for/with whom I work; others see me as indispensable and helpful.

Gain Status and Recognition
I am appreciated and admired for my talents and abilities. I am grateful for all comments I receive about my work, whether they are praising/positive or not.

Make a Contribution
I serve others with gratitude and appreciate every opportunity to make a contribution, large or small, to others with whom I interact today.

Money and Comfort
I work in a job that values me fairly for all that I bring. I am accumulating wealth to make life comfortable for me and those I love.

Chapter 5
Letting Go (Detachment and Trust)

If you stand straight, do not fear a crooked shadow.
—Chinese Proverb

Never hire or promote in your own image. It is foolish to replicate your strength and idiotic to replicate your weakness. It is essential to employ, trust, and reward those whose perspective, ability, and judgment are radically different from yours. It is also rare, for it requires uncommon humility, tolerance and wisdom.
—Dee W. Hock (Founder & CEO Emeritus, VISA International)[1]

What do we mean by letting go? It means gaining the understanding that we can't control everything around us. It means asking others for help. Trying to control things just doesn't work. It creates anxiety, knee-jerk reactions and non-strategic thinking. We see this expressed numerous times by our clients, as well as ourselves. Perhaps the greatest lesson about letting go occurs when times get tough for corporations, and the first thing that typically gets cut is labor. Often, cutting labor is a short-term fix that is detrimental to the company, as well as the overall well-being of associates and society at large. Frequently, layoffs are done out of a need to control rather than from a *deeper understanding* of the situation.

What message does this send to a workforce about its value to the organization? Research indicates that downsizing doesn't really save costs. Instead, layoffs—especially abrupt and unanticipated ones—raise anxiety, cause insecurity and hurt employee morale, which then hurts corporate performance.[2] Often, there are alternatives to exerting this type of control that will achieve better results. This chapter provides examples of leaders who let go of control in hard times—trusting associates with the truth—then showing them support and care as they put that truth into action.

Learning from Horses

Perhaps one of the best examples of letting go and getting better results is the work of Monty Roberts, a world-renowned horse trainer. Monty grew up in a family of horse trainers. His father, like most conventional horse trainers, believed that the way to break horses is through power, dominance and fear. Monty grew up witnessing the suffering of these horses. He related to the horses' predicament because his father treated him in a similar manner. As a result, Monty set out to find a better way to break horses—to accomplish the objective of *discipline with compassion*.

Monty's father approached horse-breaking as a way of exerting power over the wild, and sometimes uncontrollable, animal in order to prove superiority and dominance. His father believed that the horse must be controlled so it would fear the rider. How did Monty find a compassionate and loving way to break horses? He let go of trying to establish power over the horse. He decided to come from a place in his heart, learning to understand the horses—to really understand their thoughts. He studied horses in the pasture for hours, observing their behavior and deciphering their communication with one another. Then, he emulated and modeled their body language in order to establish complete rapport with them. He was able, in essence, to communicate with the horses. The horses, in turn, responded to him, and trust was formed.

Letting Go of Control
(author unknown)

Letting go does not mean to stop caring; it means I can't do it for someone else.

Letting go is not to cut myself off; it's the realization that I can't control another.

Letting go is not to enable, but to allow learning from natural consequences.

Letting go is to admit powerlessness, which means the outcome is not in my hands.

Letting go is not to try to change or blame another; it's to make the most of myself.

Letting go is not to care for, but to care about; it's to allow another to be a human being.

Letting go is not to be in the middle, arranging all the outcomes; it's to allow others to affect their own destinies.

Letting go is not to be protective; it's to permit another to face reality; it's not to deny, but to accept.

Letting go is not to nag, scold, or argue, but to search out my own shortcomings and correct them.

Letting go is not to adjust everything to my desires, but to take each day as it comes and cherish myself in it.

Letting go is not to criticize and regulate anybody, but to try to become what I dream I can be.

Letting go is not to regret the past, but to grow and live for the future. Letting go is to fear less and love more.[3]

Today, Monty successfully breaks horses in a quarter of the time required by traditional methods. Monty has gone on to train numerous horses, horse owners and trainers. The horses that he trains do not fear humans, and it is reported that the horses have a relationship of mutual trust with their riders. Once and for all, Monty proved that an animal does not need to be physically dominated or abused to respond effectively. How long did it take him to learn the language of the horses? How long did it take to build the trust between man and animal? Monty spent hours observing the horses, investing a lot of time. He was willing to spend the time necessary to really understand each animal, to show the animal tremendous love and respect, to honor its existence as being as worthy as his own, and to make a connection.

Because Monty was willing to invest the time up front, give up control, be more strategic in accomplishing his goal, and be patient and focused on his outcome, he was successful. Not with force—not with power—but with love, compassion and patience. How successful has he been with this approach? He has transformed horses on which others have given up. He is successful at taming wild mustangs, which all in the horse community agree is next to impossible. He got the attention of the Queen of England and has taken care of her horses in the process.

How does Monty's work with horses relate to heart-centered leadership? In times of economic hardship, recession or strong competition, some leaders argue they don't have the time to sit and observe and take note; they feel they need to take immediate action. As a leader, you can bet you will spend the time either up front or at the back end cleaning up the mess made by trying to control everything around you. Haven't you experienced this? Monty spends all of his time up front.

Trusting Employees with the Truth

The previous chapter described the importance of authenticity, of telling the truth and understanding that employees need what you need. *Telling the truth* is the first step; the next is to *trust others with the truth*, trust them to do the right thing with the truth.

In Susan's past experience as general manager of a major hotel chain, she faced an amazing financial challenge. Her hotel was about $80,000 ahead of plan in revenue, so she thought her hotel was in good shape. It was August, and the company was on track to exceed all financial goals by year's end. Then Susan learned that the partial owners of the hotel had been promised a return larger than $80,000. There were six hotels in which these owners had a partial financial interest—Susan's hotel and five others. Each of the six managers had to find a way to generate significant increase in revenue between August and December of that year. This was a monumental task, based on the sales that had been booked for the remaining four months, and winter is typically the slowest season of the year. Susan had a decision to make that would affect all her associates. She worried: *"How much do I tell them? How much should I share about why we are about to experience some dramatic cuts in expenses? How do I do the right thing and support our company's initiative, while explaining to my associates what we are about to experience?"*

After much deliberation, Susan decided to tell the truth. She met with people from each department, asked for their help, asked them to assist her in reaching the goals, and asked them to assist with a voluntary reduction of hours. She shared with all associates the following: *"We committed to our owners a dollar amount of profit that perhaps was unrealistic, but we committed to it anyway. You deserve great recognition for the amount of extra revenue that we have already generated this year."* Susan showed her associates the math and educated them on what the hotel needed to earn between that month and December. She asked each group of associates: *"Tell me what you think we can do to cut costs and raise revenue. What would you do if you were in my shoes?"* Susan put up revenue goals so all could see the progress toward reaching their goals.

The experience was unbelievable—these associates greatly exceeded her expectations. They pulled together and decided who in which department really needed the hours, and who didn't. Susan trusted them with these decisions. She tried to get work for them at neighboring hotels until her hotel could pull through. She worked shifts in various departments where she felt she could do the most good. There were many other things that each associate was willing and able to do.

So why were Susan's associates motivated to reach the financial goals, even when it meant a reduction in hours? We truly believe they did so because Susan told the truth, and she let go and trusted them to find the way. Susan gave them tremendous respect by showing that, no matter their position (most were non-English speaking and technically uneducated), she trusted them with this important information, and she trusted they could handle the truth.

In the end, her hotel accomplished the goal. Sure, there was a lot of pain along the way. For example, it took more than a year to regain market share, and customer service scores decreased by approximately 20 percent. Ultimately the company realized that the demand for increased revenue was unrealistic, short-term thinking. However, the lesson of trusting employees with the truth—honoring and respecting all individuals to understand what everyone (we) needed to do—made the experience worthwhile. When associates are trusted to do the right thing, they feel a part of the team; they know they have a leader who deeply understands "they need what you need." As a result, all get together and focus on what "we need."

From Letting Go to Serving

Letting go of control can be a very powerful teacher to a leader who is practicing the other principles described in this book. First, you learn to tell the truth. Then you can learn to trust your associates with the truth. But you must also show sincerity and a deep care for them.

When we interviewed Perry Sorenson, COO of Outrigger Hotels & Resorts, he stressed the importance of the combination of showing trust and care: "I think it is absolutely critical that a leader communicate and be very sincere and walk the talk. Being very sincere is so important. The leader must show a genuine concern and have care for his people."

We asked Perry how he is able to demonstrate this. His response, and the following story, show that a leader can handle a difficult situation by listening, letting go and showing care:

Here in Hawaii, when the first Gulf War took place, it was a crisis situation that forced us to be creative. Our business was severely impacted, in part because ours is a vacation destination. We went from 90 percent demand down to 60 percent. We knew that we were going to have to make some very tough decisions. So we took this opportunity to look at who we are as a company. We asked ourselves, 'What do we stand for? Why do people come to Hawaii and stay with us?' And we looked at why our associates chose to work with us instead of any number of competitors. We decided that our people really embodied the spirit of Hawaii, and the spirit of hospitality. So we started a process to improve our business. First, we made sure that all of our people understood the tradition of Hawaii. We determined that we wanted to be part of the community. And that we wanted each and every associate to feel really welcomed and a part of our company. We are very fortunate to have very low turnover, and, because our team members had been with us a long time, they could give us some very insightful information. We asked them, 'When we are operating at our best what are we doing? What are our values? What is precious to us?' From these discussions we created our values, not management-driven values, but associate-driven values.

Notice that, in the face of a crisis, the effective leader does not rein in control. Although there was a substantial drop in business, and some reduction in hours and work opportunity, there was a renewed focus on enlisting the strengths of the people to ensure their company survived. As Perry says:

I feel my job is to protect what they created. I believe there are times in life that one goes through an epiphany. This was one of those times. The tremendous loyalty that was built was incredible to see. A leader must build trust. I just truly care about people, and it doesn't matter the associate's title. You need outstanding housemen just like you need outstanding general managers. It is so important for a leader to understand how important people are. You must show interest, genuine interest; if you don't really care, they can tell.

Of interest is that after 10 years, the values still survive, unamended, and are a cornerstone of our relationships, not only with our company Ohana (family), but also with customers, owners and the communities where we do business. I think caring for people, treating them with respect, and being truthful have really helped us through the many storms that have followed that time—recessions, 9/11, wars, SARS, etc.

The important message is the leader builds trust by listening, letting go and not having to make all the decisions. Perry Sorenson may have

> Leaders must be able to move human hearts—to challenge people and make them want to scale steep peaks.
> —Warren Bennis and James O'Toole
> (*Harvard Business Review*, May-June 2000)[4]

guided the associates, but ultimately he was able to let go when he asked them to help figure out a solution. To be trusted, you must trust. In the process of letting go, Perry Sorenson witnessed—had an epiphany about—the power of the "human element." Given the opportunity, people created and acted out of their own values. In the end, heart-centered leadership involves serving your associates, "and it doesn't matter the associate's title." The outcome was an increased differentiation from the competition, a new and successful marketing strategy and sustained retention.

Heart-Centered Leadership: Integration of Core Principles

Are you beginning to see a holistic synergy of the different virtues for heart-centered leadership? Let's revisit the idea that the principles work together, even though this book treats them separately.

Both Susan and Perry describe stories of crisis, and how associates rose to the occasion when they were told the truth and trusted. The ability to let go doesn't arise by itself. All the principles work together. The commitment to personal growth (know thyself), open-mindedness (don't judge) and authenticity (they need what you need) are all involved in the ability to detach and trust (letting go). The heart-centered leader appears to embody all these principles within a holistic collective.

The following is an interview we conducted with Sharon Wibben, senior vice president of in-flight service at Delta Air Lines. The interview sheds a great deal of insight on the various principles of heart-centered leadership that we have discussed thus far. This interview is important because it shows how all the different principles work together as a whole. They are integrated and flow into each other. To let go, a leader has to admit that he or she needs help and can't do it alone. To refrain from judgment, a leader has to know what it is like to do the job of those he or she leads.

As you read this interview, try to imagine what Sharon is like as a "whole" person and assess how she integrates the principles.

Interviewer: What do you think is the role of a leader today?
Sharon: It is modeling the behavior that we want people to emulate. We, as leaders, all know firsthand what it feels like to work with people that we really respect. I feel I have to look in the mirror and ask myself, 'Am I modeling the right behavior?'

Interviewer: What are the right behaviors?
Sharon: Honesty, openness, respect, taking time with people. Really focusing on your audience. I have learned that the higher up you go, the more important this is, to get clear on your audience. You have to be able to communicate effectively. As you move up the ladder, you seem to get very limited time with people. It is condensed to sound bites, [so] you'd better be able to communicate very well in sound bites. In those few sound bites, you have to be able to influence behavior.

I also think that it is the value system. We lose sight sometimes; the real leader is one people can trust. Someone you can count on and anticipate some consistency—who can take away the mystery.

Interviewer: How do you do this?
Sharon: It happens every day, especially when you come into an organization, are new to the organization and new to the industry. You have to earn people's trust, and you have to earn credibility. This has never failed me, this understanding.

You have to be very clear about your vision and then communicate that vision. You have to gain understanding of what your people are dealing with.

Interviewer: How have you done that?
Sharon: I spent a lot of time traveling around and listening to the issues, concerns and ideas. I also went through flight attendant training myself, graduated and got my wings. I wanted to understand what the flight attendants face. I also gained a great sense of Delta's culture.

After this experience, I wrote my vision, pulled my extended team together (peers and such), ran it by them, and asked for their input and thoughts. A month later it was completed, and I knew I had to bridge the gap among the flight attendants and me. I was committed to meet with each of the 20,000 flight attendants. I held 52 different sessions throughout the country and just put myself out there.

Interviewer: What was the agenda and purpose for these meetings?

Sharon: I wanted to communicate our vision. I wanted them to be able to have an open dialogue with me. I wanted them to be able to ask any question they wanted. I wanted them to get to know me as their leader. I wanted them to know what they could expect from me, and I wanted them to know what I expected of them. I also shared my observations from all that I had experienced. Some of these meetings were tough. But the critical point was that we got connected.

Interviewer: What was the result?

Sharon: Unbelievable. When people saw me doing this, it became the foundation for us to move forward; there was more to come. To this day, people are still talking about this.

I also think a good leader stays the course. Create the vision; stay the course; be clear on expectations. I think a leader has to have a great deal of courage; a good support system. Psychological health. It is lonely at the top, so these things are important. It also takes a great deal of courage. You have to be able to pull from deep within yourself at times, because we only do the best we know how. I have a tremendous faith in God. This faith helps me immensely, as does the support from my family. As the job gets bigger, the more responsibility you have to do it right—to make the right decisions.

Sometimes people don't or can't admit they need help. It is okay to reveal that you don't know how to do something. It takes self-confidence to do this, though. Maybe they have been conditioned in their lives to feel it is not safe, or okay to admit they don't know.

I believe that people just want to do a good job, even if their behavior doesn't look that way. I guess some people can get to the point where they don't care anymore.

The other thing I see is that people have so much potential, and they or we don't realize it. It's the whole Pygmalion effect. We have a responsibility to create the proper environment, the learning organization, and tap into the creativity of our people. This philosophy has never failed me.

Interviewer: Why do you think people get to the point of not caring anymore?

Sharon: It could be personal things in their life, but we have to be mindful of what kind of environment we are creating, and they are creating for themselves. The leader's job is to remove the barriers, enable the proper behavior, and then it is up to the individual. This will work as long as we are airtight on how consistently we are providing what they need. It takes capability, the right approach and commitment from all parties. There is too much victim mentality.

Interviewer: How much do the actions of a leader affect the motives of his or her associates?

Sharon: Maybe 70 percent if not higher [felt it was higher after some thought]. You, as the leader, need to know who you are as a person. Who we are as people will determine who we are as leaders. It is the inside-out approach. How can we say 'empower your people,' when we are not empowering ourselves? How can you create the environment around you? By creating the communication strategy and management processes.

You also need visible leadership. Sitting in the office behind the desk can't do it. Be ready to be challenged. We also must inspect what we expect, and catch people doing it right.

Interviewer: Was there a turning point in your life that caused you to have the leadership philosophy that you have today?

Sharon: Not really. But I saw how my mother treated people, cared about people. My husband has the same qualities.

As you can tell, Sharon is dedicated to speaking the truth, to letting go and asking for help, to being authentic and to walking the talk ("Am I modeling the right behavior?"). She knows her impact on others, and, while she can help create a positive environment, she knows that associates have a choice to realize their potential in that environment. Sharon also seems to know her limits, placing importance on psychological health, finding the right support, and having spirituality or religion in her life (faith in God). The following chapters explore the additional principles of knowing your impact, realizing employees have a choice and self-care.

A Story About Letting Go

There is an often-told story about a man who hiked up a mountain and accidentally fell over a cliff. This is an interesting story because there are different versions with different endings. In each version, the man grabbed on to a branch growing out of the side of the mountain, fortunately breaking his fall. Each version tells that the man holds onto the fragile branch for dear life, his feet dangling in the space below. He hung in midair, not knowing how long he could keep his strength up. He knew that he was not far from the ridge where he fell. It is at this point that the different versions of the story diverge.

Version 1: He knew he was close enough to the cliff for anyone who might be on the mountain to hear. He was afraid of falling and afraid of looking down. So he began to yell, "Anyone up there? Help! Please, help me! Hey! Help! Please, anyone, please help me! Is there anyone up there?" An answer came, "I am here." The desperate man then cried, "Who are you? Can you help me?" Another answer came back: "I am the Lord. Just let go of the branch so that I can help you." There was a moment of silence. Then the man cried out, "Is there anyone else up there?"

Version 2: Just as he realized the predicament he was in, the man noticed that a large rat had begun to gnaw on the branch—making his situation even worse. At the next moment, he saw that there was a large clump of ripe berries growing on a bush within arm's reach. The man—who, it is told, was an enlightened saint or guru—used his free arm to begin eating the berries. He ate each berry one at a time; taking his time to look at each berry, to consider its color, ripeness and texture.

Version 3: Not long after the man's fall, a hiking buddy stumbled on the path and noticed his friend's sack lying at the edge of the cliff. He bent to pick it up and was stunned by the sight of his friend hanging on to the branch. In his surprise, the hiking buddy lost his balance and fell over the cliff, passing his friend on the way. The first man yelled as his friend passed, "How are you?" His friend answered, "So far, so good!"

The different endings to this story represent different perspectives on letting go, but they all point to the willingness (or lack thereof) to stay in the moment in a mindful and vigilant way. Version 1 shows how funny our relationship with God or a Higher Power can be. Sometimes, even when help is available and staring us in the face, we still look for options. Version 2 is really a meditation on the power of the moment and the ability to appreciate the present, even in the midst of seeming chaos and darkness. When things are not going our way, the unenlightened response is to get agitated, worry and fret, and flail about— to the point where our own mindless actions will cause the branch to break. Version 3 makes the same point, but more dramatically, and offers the element of hope: "so far, so good." Part of letting go is recognizing that, even when we feel doomed, there is the possibility of another branch or cliff up ahead to break our fall.

Exercise for "Letting Go"

In understanding letting go, it is helpful to know how much of your situation is affected by your own attitudes about control, such as difficulty trusting, being a perfectionist, having unrealistic expectations or harboring an illusion of control when you really have none. It is also important to know how much flexibility or job latitude your work position or environment gives you. Too often, we confuse these two things: our need, and what our job offers. In this exercise, we ask that you assess (1) how much your need for control gets in the way of things, (2) how much you work in a position that does or doesn't afford you the amount of control that you need, and (3) the degree of match between the freedom in your job and your need for discretion and latitude at work. You have to be honest with yourself to answer the following questions. The point of this exercise is to look deeply at how much you are able and willing to let go.

For each item addressed in the chart below, indicate on a four-point scale whether the item is (1) very untrue, (2) somewhat untrue, (3) somewhat true or (4) very true.

My Need for Control	Score	Control in My Job	Score
I would rather work on important tasks than delegate or count on others to do them right.		I have a great deal of say over how things are done at my job.	
I feel pressured to meet the standards I have set.		My job gives me flexibility to be creative in how and when work gets done.	
It is difficult for me to trust associates or co-workers with tasks I know I can do better.		There is enough time in the day to complete all the tasks I need to do at work.	
I analyze how to keep things under better control at work.		Procedures/regulations at work are more helpful than restricting.	
I often look for mistakes in projects that others have completed.		My work allows time to take breaks and rest as I need to.	
I prefer tasks where I am the one who is in control of the outcome, rather than tasks requiring group coordination.		The lines of communication at work allow me to easily contact others if and when I need their input.	
I often feel I am working with people who are incompetent.		People can progress in this organization if they are effective.	
People tell me I need to let go or that I need too much control.		I can decide on my own how to go about doing my work.	
Total Your Need Score (Possible LOW of 8 and HIGH of 32)		Total Your Job Score (Possible LOW of 8 and HIGH of 32)	

Figure 5.1

Assessing Yourself: If your Need Score is *greater than* 20, your need for control may be unrealistic. A score *greater than* 27 suggests an unrealistic and unhealthy need for control. If your Job Score is *less than* 20, you are working in a job that may be stressful. If it is *less than* 12, your job offers extremely little control and may be unhealthy.

Also, if your Need Score is 4 to 8 points higher than your Job Score, your need for control is not well-matched to your position. If your Need Score is 8 or more points higher, you are working in a stressful situation, and you will likely benefit from reading the chapter "Care for the Heart" (see Chapter 8).

Generally speaking, a healthy ability to let go is indicated when any of the following three conditions exist: (1) your Need Score is relatively low (less than 15), (2) your Job Score is relatively high (greater than 25) or (3) your Job Score is higher than your Need Score.

Chapter 6
*Know the Impact of Your Words and Actions
(Integrity/Foresight)*

> *Forethought and prudence are the proper qualities of a leader.*
> —Tacitus

> *In looking for people to hire, you look for three qualities: integrity, intelligence, and energy.*
> *And if they don't have the first, the other two will kill you.*
> —Warren Buffett, CEO, Berkshire Hathaway, Inc.[1]

> *Sometimes, when you are a Bear of Very Little Brain, and you Think of Things,*
> *you find sometimes that a Thing which seemed very Thingish inside you is quite different*
> *when it gets out into the open and has other people looking at it.*
> —Winnie-the-Pooh

As leaders, we underestimate the impact that we have on others. Everything we do and say, as well as what we don't do and say, is observed by our team members. And, based on their observations, associates make decisions, judge and—sometimes hastily—draw conclusions about you. This is a very challenging position to be in, for we are human. And humans are fallible. We make mistakes. As we strive to have a positive impact, it is helpful to remember the values of integrity and foresight. We must make a fundamental decision to act in accord with deeply held values, to practice what we preach and have the foresight to think through the consequences of our actions.

When you act with integrity and foresight, your impact as a leader may extend beyond your associates. This chapter also explores your impact on customers, the work climate, suppliers, the community and colleagues outside your organization, as well as on your own leadership career. So when we talk about "knowing your impact," we ask you to think of all the people you affect in your job.

We equate the role of a leader in an organization to that of a fish in a fishbowl. You, as leader, swim around minding your own business and doing what you need to do. Meanwhile, the rest of the world views you through the glass. Indeed, as in a fishbowl, they magnify your actions or blow them out of proportion. Your associates rarely see things from your perspective, while your job—in knowing your impact—is to try to see things from their perspective. What a challenging position to be in! Every day, leaders are subject to the "fishbowl effect."

The Fishbowl Effect

Below we have listed some ways in which the "fishbowl" effect can produce both positive and negative impressions. Specifically, we have observed how ordinary actions can leave long-lasting impressions.

- You are an executive, and your only acceptable choice of transportation to and from the airport while attending the company conference is a limousine. What message does this send to the conference attendees? What is your impact?
- When you personally show up to greet new associates at the company orientation, what message does this send? What is your impact?
- When you kick off the company's conference with a speech that you have not practiced or rehearsed, what message does this send? What is your impact?
- When you send a handwritten note to an associate, thanking him or her for outstanding performance, what message does this send? What is your impact?
- When you arrange town hall meetings for associates to attend, as a way to communicate more effectively, what message does this send? What is your impact?
- When you bad-mouth an associate in front of others, what message does this send? What is your impact?
- When you publicly show genuine gratitude for an associate's contribution, what message does this send? What is your impact?
- When you are not present for the associate picnic or holiday party, what message does this send? What is your impact?

The list goes on and on. This chapter will help you understand that as a leader, you make an impact every day. The question is, what impact do you want to make? Heart-centered leadership involves taking the perspective of your associates and attempting to understand how your actions affect them.

What does that mean? First, we are not talking about dramatic actions, such as downsizing or mergers, new product launches or major changes in structure or strategy. Of course your impact is felt there. We refer more to the impact you make every day—your typical style or your way of relating. Second, we are not suggesting that you walk on eggshells. Being in the fishbowl means you are allowed to make mistakes and recover. Third, when we talk abut "knowing" your impact, we are talking not only about informational knowledge, such as returns on investment or bottom-line calculations. We refer more to a *heartfelt or empathetic understanding* of how you (specifically and directly) come across in your dealings with others.

The Climate of Training and Learning: From Fishbowl to Aquarium

Perhaps the clearest and most important example of how leaders impact associates is in their understanding of the work climate or the "social ecology" of the workplace. To build on the fishbowl metaphor, a heart-centered leader doesn't stay in the bowl. Instead, he or she gets out a lot, mingles in the aquarium, studies and acts on the situations which develop daily. This movement is particularly helpful whenever a company is investing in new training and development initiatives, whether they are customer service training workshops or large-scale quality improvement or culture changes.

Our firm designed and implemented a customer service initiative for a large service company. One of the key components of this training was to help the leaders of this organization understand the importance of the climate surrounding training. Research suggests that this climate is often crucial to the success of training and to the realization of a return on the investment. So we discussed the leader's impact during the training and the importance of showing genuine interest during the process.

You would think that when an organization makes a considerable investment in training, leaders would automatically show this genuine interest. After all, companies pay good money for it! Unfortunately, more often than not, leaders underestimate the impact of their behaviors and actions on the success of the training initiative.

It was recommended that these senior leaders inquire about the training each time they visited their stores. Leaders can have a positive effect simply by asking associates' opinions of the training. What impact did these leaders have on the training experience? It soon hit the grapevine that the leaders were discussing the training initiative. This underlined the importance of the training, further engaging not only the associates who attended the training, but their supervisors as well. A satisfactory result was brought about by simply inquiring about the training initiative, at no additional time or cost. Know your impact.

While writing this book, we studied other examples of the effects of the climate surrounding training, and the results were similar. One example involved training in Total Quality (TQ) Management for a large public organization. The program was rolled out differently in each department, depending on the choice and interest of the department head. As you might expect, some work group supervisors were enthusiastic and supportive of the new training. Other supervisors saw the training as an extra burden. In an extreme case, a few supervisors created "TQ my way or the highway," which failed to empower associates as prescribed by the TQ philosophy. A key finding of this study was that those associates who were trained in TQ, *but* who lacked a supportive climate, indicated worse performance than those who had never been trained. Alternately, trained associates who had supportive leadership performed better than those not trained. Of course, supervisors were more encouraging when the department head also supported TQ. Know your impact!

Companies invest considerable efforts in training associates and in culture change programs. We contend—from both consultation and scientific study—that this investment is often a waste of time and money because leadership fails to support the effort from start to finish. In short, heart-centered leaders must *stay connected* to the larger environment or climate surrounding the development of associates. The added benefit is that you will not only know your impact, but you will also reduce wasted time and effort.

Integrity and Foresight as Risk Management

We coached a client named Robert—a senior vice president of a large corporation—in preparation for a speech. The organization had grown significantly, and many managers attending the conference had not had an opportunity to meet Robert. He knew that his presentation skills needed significant improvement and hired us to help. Our first question in preparing Robert for this assignment really stumped him. We asked, "What do you want this audience to think, know and feel about you at the end of the speech?" Robert had never thought about his impact, and he assumed that the coaching would focus strictly on helping him develop his message.

Although engaging content is necessary for a good presentation, we believe it is more critical for a leader to anticipate his or her personal impact on the audience. In coaching for heart-centered leadership, leaders must decide what effect they want to achieve, and then build from there. The reality is that some type of impact will be made, but what kind? We often see this failure to think through our impact as a major blind spot for leaders. Of course, this impact goes beyond the content of the speech—and even the delivery—to show we interact with and relate to associates.

After much thought, Robert decided he wanted the audience to think he was extremely professional, confident and credible. He wanted the audience to know that this organization was in good hands. Using this as a guiding principle, we began our work together so that Robert would deliver an outstanding speech. And, indeed, he did just that! It seemed the goals of the coaching had been clearly accomplished, as members of the audience gave him favorable ratings after the speech. Unfortunately, there is more to this story.

Later that evening, the company held an awards banquet. Due to the size of the room and the number of attendees, they used television cameras and large screens to bring the leaders on stage closer to the audience. A number of screens were mounted around the room. Apparently, Robert had a few too many drinks, and his drunken appearance and slurring of words were broadcast for all to see. What was his impact now? How did it differ from the one he had created earlier in his speech? What final impact did the audience take with them? Recall the impact that Robert wanted to make was one of professionalism, credibility and confidence. His hours of practice and rehearsal went down the drain in a split second. Although Robert professed certain values, his actions didn't support these values—he lacked integrity—and he did not anticipate the consequences of his drinking—he lacked foresight. This is why integrity and foresight go hand in hand with the principle, "Know your impact."

The Rippling Effects of Respect

We interviewed Perry Sorenson for this book partly because of the impact he had on Susan as a young, inexperienced general manager. For many reasons, Perry's leadership stands out clearly in Susan's mind. Her story:

> *Although Perry was not my immediate boss, he was the COO of the organization, who communicated with the general managers on a periodic basis. One day, Perry called to congratulate me on our latest profit-and-loss statement, and asked me what I was doing to make such significant increases in room rates and profitability. It meant a lot to receive a personal call from him, and receive his recognition. When you work hard to produce good results, it is nice to know that*

your work is noticed. That made an impact on me, but the following conversation meant even more. Perry asked me if it would be possible to get a room in our hotel for a weekend trip he was planning with his wife. Notice that he didn't say, 'I'm coming down, get me a room.' Instead, he asked if it would be possible to get a room. This is the COO of the organization talking! Needless to say, it was more than possible. His approach was so respectful that I was sincerely motivated to make sure that he not only had a room, but the best one in the house!

This story gets better. During their weekend trip, Perry and his wife purchased a gift and left it on my desk for me to find when I came in to work on Monday morning. The gift was accompanied by a 'Thank You' card expressing their gratitude for my hospitality. Needless to say, this made an impact. In the busy pace of the business world, the fact that he didn't demand a room was impressive enough; but to genuinely thank me for something that he could have rightfully expected of me as a general manager was something special. When was the last time that you requested, versus demanded, something of an associate? When was the last time you genuinely thanked an associate for doing his job? So did Perry create an impact? Yes, in fact that incident happened 14 years ago, and I remember it every time I think of him as a leader. Know your impact.

The importance of leaders treating associates with respect—especially in service industries—must not be underestimated, particularly for its ultimate impact on consumers, guests and customers. Knowing your impact also extends beyond your associates—to suppliers (both internal and external), current customers and future markets. Consider the recent book by Fred Crawford and Ryan Mathews, *The Myth of Excellence*.[2]

In their survey research, Crawford and Mathews found that an increasing number of consumers are interested in *values* (respect, honesty, trust and dignity), more so than *value*. That is, customers want to be treated with respect—they want to feel that the process of service has a positive impact on their personal selves—perhaps more so than the value or utility of a given product. In a recent interview in *Fast Company* magazine, Mathews, a futurist who studies trends in consumer behavior, noted: "It's not just the value that you're offering the customer; it's the values of the store, reflected in the way the store does business. What people told us was, "We want to do business with people who are fair and honest. We want to do business with people who respect us as individuals. Don't give us phony discounts. Don't give us a fake smile. Don't have a greeter at the door who's there like a zombie, pretending to welcome us, but who's really checking for shoplifters."[3]

In other words, customers—just like associates—want to be treated with integrity. They want to know that you have taken the time to think about *their* experience and have prepared accordingly. This is not merely a marketing strategy. Were we to treat it as such, customers would sense it, just like associates know when we are not being authentic (see Chapter 4). Indeed, knowing your impact requires insight into the surrounding situation and the future context that ripples outward from your actions. As we said earlier, leaders may operate in a fishbowl, but they affect others.

Like the work climate, the context is critical to the success of many operations. Indeed, researchers have studied "contextual performance," or ways in which associates cooperate with internal and external suppliers of services. These researchers note that positive impact is more likely when associates have the ability to take the perspective of their suppliers, when they have empathy for them and positive attributes about them.[4]

This study suggests that we might be able to break the "know your impact" principle into several components:

- Your interaction with associates
- Your capacity to empathize with associates
- Understanding how your actions contribute to the whole

The exercise portion of this chapter includes a guided self-assessment to help you determine your strengths and needs with respect to these three components. In short, it all comes down to respect and cooperation. When Perry Sorenson treated Susan this way, she was more likely to be cooperative and better able to understand the perspectives of those she served.

Impact as Leaders Move Up

The ability to influence, persuade and negotiate is essential to moving up the ladder in an organization. We once coached a top-level director of a large pharmaceutical company who had been promoted to a new position—we will call her Jan. Jan had risen very quickly in the organization, as she had in all the previous organizations for which she had worked. We started working together because Jan received feedback from her peers and boss that she was not doing well at building relationships in the organization. She was not successful in influencing, persuading and negotiating with her peers to take a certain course of action. This started to derail Jan's career and, until she was given this feedback, she was not aware of her impact, and certainly not aware how pervasive this impact was on her and her team's ability to do its work.

We are happy to report that, as of today, Jan is well on her way to working through this issue. This is because she was willing to assess the cause of her problems working with her peers. Jan's problems stemmed from the rapid climb in her career and the effect this had on her values and principles. Her problems related to everything in this book. First of all, she didn't know herself. She had a number of personal barriers (self- judgment and anxiety) that were obstacles to effectively working with others. She also judged her peers a great deal instead of trying to understand their needs and issues. She didn't understand that her peers basically needed the same things she did. Jan felt that her peers had negative intentions when they communicated with her. She did not understand the way they chose to work with her. She didn't realize that the way she communicated with them was creating very negative impact.

So who cares? What is the danger in this? After all, she was a high performer. As with other leaders who move up the ladder too quickly, Jan's status as a high performer rapidly sank because she was not sensitive to the climate, context and impact of her actions. She was unable to get cooperation from her peers and, therefore, discovered that she couldn't get anything done. In her position, as in most organizations, her success was directly related to her being able to work effectively with other key departments. Slowly but surely, Jan placed herself in a position of being totally unproductive. As you might have guessed, her behavior filtered down to her associates as well. Jan quickly lost ground with her team and became ineffective at motivating, inspiring or influencing them to do good work.

Pride

In telling Jan's story, we should clarify that her problems did not stem from self-righteousness or pride so much as from her inability to "read the field"—to be sensitive to her new aquarium. Perhaps a bigger barrier to "knowing your impact" is pride, stubbornness or self-determination to do things your own way, regardless of what others might think. As leaders, we each create an impact every minute of every day. Decisions are made about us as leaders, and impressions are formed. These impressions include how you are perceived by others.

Recently, we attended a client's national sales conference, where a group of star performers was asked to participate in a panel discussion. The discussion centered on the panel members sharing best practices. In other words, what were they doing to be effective in sales? Most of the panel members were polished and professional. However, we couldn't help but notice one particular panel member. He came across as prideful and arrogant, almost as though the audience of sales managers should feel lucky to be in his presence. Needless to say, he ended up losing a great deal of credibility in a short amount of time. The audience left saying, "He may be effective in sales, but I question his integrity in the process." To be sure, this gentleman was touted as one of the best salespersons in the organization, but, in less than 30 minutes, he lost tremendous respect within his sales community.

In another example, we witnessed a CEO screaming at his general managers at an operations conference. He was very frustrated with the managers' performance and communicated that frustration in no uncertain terms. As a result this particular CEO lost a great deal of credibility. Worse yet, his objective to motivate this group of operators to perform at higher levels significantly backfired. Again, this harks back to the principle "Know thyself." When you are angry about something, it is not the best time to talk with—much less yell or scream at—someone about the issue.

Adaptability and Feedback

The stories in this chapter suggest that the ability to know your impact requires a willingness to get feedback about your behavior and to adapt or modify your actions on the basis of this feedback. Why bother knowing your impact if you don't care enough to change your behavior? That's the problem with pride, and if you've successfully climbed the corporate ladder, you may believe there is no need to change. This is where Jan had a problem adapting. Knowing your impact can threaten your previous view of yourself.

The importance of adaptability and feedback is shown clearly in Robert E. Kaplan's book *Character Shifts: The Challenge of Improving Executive Performance Through Personal Growth.*[5] This study indicated that, even when executives want to know their impact, there are often social norms against providing feedback to highly placed and accomplished individuals. Associates may be fearful of a backlash and are, therefore, generally not willing to tell it like it is. Executives need to appear competent and, like all of us, adopt a personal strategy which enables them to maintain self-esteem. Kaplan explains that in order to keep growing, executives must change their behavior as well as their character or personality.

Concluding Points

In Chapter 1, we discussed power and influence. We hope it is clear from this chapter that "knowing your impact" has to do with your willingness to put your power needs aside for the sake of having a genuine influence on others. When you are caught up in having things your way—when you feel that you can't let go—it is probably a signal that you do not know your impact, or that you may soon lose the ground you have gained.

We once conducted a study in which student participants were asked to lead others in a discussion and help them reach consensus on a decision.[6] As the time to make a final decision approached, some students became increasingly antagonistic, their blood pressure actually rising, and were seen as less effective by group participants. Other students relaxed and became more supportive and were seen as more effective. The key difference between these two types of student was in their basic desire to have either power (to enjoy positions of dominance) or to have influence (to make a difference and enjoy influencing opinions). This study—a basic message of this chapter—is that heart-centered leaders understand how their own motives can get in the way of having a positive influence. So knowing your impact involves knowing your motives and being willing to act from a position of consensus-building and positive influence.

Knowing Your Impact: A True Story

We chose the following story, written by Jeff McMullen, because it speaks directly to the values of integrity and foresight of both which are integral to knowing your impact. Jeff is a motivational speaker and consultant. You can reach him at www.jeffmcmullen.com.

> A number of years ago (1983–1987), I had the opportunity to play the character of Ronald McDonald for the McDonald's Corporation. One of our standard events was Ronald Day. One day each month, we visited as many of the community hospitals as possible, bringing a little happiness into a place where no one ever looks forward to going. I was very proud to be able to make a difference for children and adults who were experiencing some downtime. The warmth and gratification I would receive stayed with me for weeks. I loved the project, McDonald's loved the project, the kids and adults loved it, and so did the nursing and hospital staffs.
>
> There were two restrictions placed on me during a visit. First, I could not go anywhere in the hospital without McDonald's personnel (my handlers), as well as hospital personnel. That way, if I were to walk into a room and frighten a child, there was someone there to address the issue immediately. And second,

I could not physically touch anyone within the hospital. They did not want me transferring germs from one patient to another. I understood why they had this "don't touch" rule, but I didn't like it. I believe that touching is the most honest form of communication we will ever know. Printed and spoken words can lie; it is impossible to lie with a warm hug.

Breaking either of these rules, I was told, meant I could lose my job.

Toward the end of my fourth year of "Ronald Days," as I was heading down a hallway after a long day in greasepaint and on my way home, I heard a little voice. "Ronald, Ronald." I stopped. The soft little voice was coming through a half-open door. I pushed the door open and saw a young boy, about five years old, lying in his dad's arms, hooked up to more medical equipment than I had ever seen.

Mom was on the other side, along with Grandma, Grandpa and a nurse tending to the equipment. I knew by the feeling in the room that the situation was grave. I asked the little boy his name—he told me it was Billy—and I did a few simple magic tricks for him. As I stepped back to say good-bye, I asked Billy if there was anything else I could do for him.

"Ronald, would you hold me?" — such a simple request. But what ran through my mind was that, if I touched him, I could lose my job. So I told Billy I could not do that right now, but I suggested that he and I color a picture. Upon completing a wonderful piece of art that we were both very proud of, Billy again asked me to hold him. By this time my heart was screaming "Yes!" But my mind was screaming louder. "No! You are going to lose your job!"

This second time that Billy asked me, I had to ponder why I could not grant the simple request of a little boy who probably would not be going home. I asked myself why was I being logically and emotionally torn apart by someone I had never seen before and probably would never see again. "Hold me." It was such a simple request, and yet ... I searched for any reasonable response that would allow me to leave. I could not come up with a single one. It took me a moment to realize that in this situation, losing my job may not be the disaster I feared.

Was losing my job the worst thing in the world? Did I have enough self-belief that if I did lose my job, I would be able to pick up and start again?

The answer was a loud, bold affirming "yes!" I could pick up and start again. So what was the risk? Just that if I lost my job, it probably would not *be long before I would lose first my car, then my home ... and to be honest with you, I really liked those things. But I realized that at the end of my life, the car would have no value and neither would the house. The only things that had steadfast value were experiences.*

Once I reminded myself that the real reason I was there was to bring a little happiness to an unhappy environment, I realized I really faced no risk at all—I sent Mom, Dad, Grandma and Grandpa out of the room, and my two McDonald's escorts out to the van. The nurse tending the medical equipment stayed, but Billy asked her to stand and face the corner.

Then I picked up this little wonder of a human being. He was so frail and so scared. We laughed and cried for 45 minutes, and talked about the things that worried him. Billy was afraid that his little brother might get lost coming home from kindergarten next year, without Billy to show him the way. He worried that his dog wouldn't get another bone because Billy had hidden the bones in the house before going back to the hospital, and now he couldn't remember where he put them. These are problems to a little boy who knows he is not going home.

On my way from the room, with tear-streaked makeup running down my neck, I gave Mom and Dad my real name and phone number (another automatic dismissal for Ronald McDonald, but I figured that I was gone and had nothing to lose), and said if there was anything the McDonald's Corporation or I could do, to give me a call and consider it done. Less than 48 hours later, I received a phone call from Billy's mom. She informed me that Billy had passed away. She and her husband simply wanted to thank me for making a difference in their little boy's life.

Billy's mom told me that shortly after I left the room, Billy looked at her and said, "Momma, I don't care anymore if I see Santa this year because I was held by Ronald McDonald." Sometimes we must do what is right for the moment, regardless of the perceived risk. Only experiences have value, and the biggest reason people limit their experiences is because of the risk involved.

For the record, McDonald's did find out about Billy and me, but, given the circumstances, permitted me to retain my job. I continued as Ronald for another year before leaving the corporation to share the story of Billy and how important it is to take risks.

Exercise for Chapter 6

This exercise is loosely based on previous research and ideas discussed in the chapter. In order to "know your impact," several things are necessary. This exercise is not designed to help you *increase* your impact. Instead, it will help you better *know* your impact. The following questions and statements are designed to help you know your impact on others. We suggest that you take an evening or two to read through and write responses to these questions and statements in your journal. Be honest with yourself about your strengths and those areas which require work. Most of the questions refer to "associates," but be aware that, at different times, the key players in heart-centered leadership are also customers, suppliers, stakeholders and the community you serve. Reflect on any or all of these players as you consider your impact. You will also note Suggested Actions under most of the capacities. If you think you need some work in these areas, we recommend trying some of these as homework.

There are three parts to this exercise. Each part will help you improve your ability to understand your associates' perspective and know your impact. There are three paths. You may find yourself drawn to one path more naturally than the others. We believe that the paths intersect, and all are required to improve your recognition of your impact. Path 1 is the *path of action* and involves interaction with associates, understanding your contribution and seeing positive intentions. Path 2 is the *path of reflection* and requires stopping to reflect, working through your actions and empathy. Path 3 is the *path of change* and involves adaptability and seeking feedback.

PATH OF ACTION

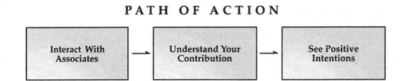

The Path of Action first requires you to *interact with associates* so that you *understand your contribution* to the successes, failures, trials and tribulations they experience. At the same time, your interaction and understanding will help you to see positive intentions in your associates (review Chapter 3).

Interaction with Associates
1. How often do you establish contact with associates? With customers? With suppliers?
2. How often do you visit the areas where associates work? Where customers do business? Where suppliers work?

The frequency of interaction is perhaps the most important factor in knowing your direct impact. As the diagram suggests, frequent interaction helps you better understand your own contribution and allows you to think positively of others.

Suggested Action: Get out, move around and spend some time hearing about how others see their work.

Understand Your Contribution
1. Do you feel you have a full understanding of how much your actions contribute to the entire work of the organization?
2. Do you understand the overall function of the organization?
3. Do you understand relationships among associates, suppliers and customers?

It's often taken for granted that leaders have an integrated understanding of how their particular jobs contribute to the overall effectiveness of the organization. However, it is possible to become disconnected from daily operations and lose sight of the leadership role, especially in regard to how your actions ultimately impact customers, suppliers and other constituents.

Suggested Actions: Conduct an associate climate survey. Ask about leadership; conduct 360-degree assessments, customer and guest satisfaction surveys, customer panels and focus groups.

See Positive Intentions

1. I believe that my associates (suppliers) are doing the best they can, given the circumstances.
2. If my associates (suppliers) make mistakes, it is not because they have bad intentions.
3. Customers who use our products/services care about the way they are treated.

Making positive attributions is one aspect of perspective-taking. By attributing positive intentions to associates, leaders are more likely to see things from the associates' perspective. This is critical to understanding how they are seen by others.

Suggested Actions: If you are overly critical of your associates, we suggest re-reading Chapter 3. It can also help to create a gratitude list and spend five minutes each day recording the qualities in your associates for which you are grateful. This exercise helps us see things in a more positive light.

PATH OF REFLECTION

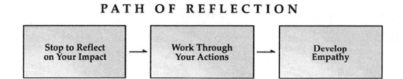

| Stop to Reflect on Your Impact | → | Work Through Your Actions | → | Develop Empathy |

The Path of Reflection first requires you to *stop and reflect on your impact* so that you *can work through the actions that contribute* to the successes, failures, trials and tribulations of your associates. Doing this will help you to *empathize* with your associates.

Stop to Reflect

1. I take time every day to review how I am seen by my associates.
2. I take time to consider exactly how I want to come across.
3. I pause during meetings to consider all the things that have been said, rather than rushing to a statement or a decision.
4. I sometimes get away from work to contemplate the many different aspects of the business.

There are three aspects to this capacity:
- Stopping or pausing;
- Activating foresight; and
- Stating desired outcomes.

Suggested Actions: You must actively pursue self-knowledge. Stop what you are doing and accept that there is virtue to working on your business as well as in your business. In order to activate foresight, ask yourself the following questions:
- *What do I want to happen?*
- *What is important to me to achieve for my associates and by my associates?*
- *Where do I want my business to be in six months? One year? Two years? Five years?*

After you take some time to really ponder these questions, you must begin to articulate the outcome you desire. Notice that this exercise is about stopping. You don't have to come up with any answers just yet. That comes later, after you get feedback.

Work Through Actions

1. How concerned are you about the actual quality of your product?
2. How concerned are you when customers are dissatisfied? When associates are dissatisfied? When suppliers are dissatisfied?
3. How often do you take time to plan or identify actions that are specific, have timelines and involve interacting with others?
4. How often do you share these planned actions with others and get their feedback?
5. How often do you get feedback from others after you execute these actions?
6. Do you monitor yourself when asking for feedback to make sure that you don't discount the feedback you get?

It's often taken for granted that leaders own the success, productivity and effectiveness of their organization. However, it is possible to become disconnected from the daily inputs, outputs, costs and investments. The "human" side of the enterprise—the satisfaction of associates, customers and others who interact with the company—especially suffers.

Working through your actions is essential for knowing your impact, because it is in the action stage that others are most likely to come into contact with you. There are three critical areas to be aware of when working through actions:

- Discounting, when you don't really listen to invited input when it is given to you.
- Trance, where you are "living in your head" because of your "high" position in the company. You think that just because you believe something is true, it really is. You spin stories about

something being done because you may have mentioned it to someone at some point (this is also called delusion or analysis-paralysis).

- Fear, where you become overwhelmed, anxious about risks and worried about exposure.

Suggested Actions: A good way to avoid "discounting" is to practice silence when another is speaking. Listen from your heart. Don't think ahead about what you will say. We suggest you spend a day just doing this. To determine whether you are in a trance, ask a coach or associate you trust to ask you this question after you talk about your ideas: "Those are wonderful thoughts, but what have you actually done with those thoughts?"

Empathy

1. I feel concerned for my associates (suppliers) if they are under pressure.
2. I understand the problems my associates (suppliers) face.
3. I feel concerned for my customers if they do not receive quality services and or have quality experiences.

Empathetic concern for others is the key ingredient to realizing a heartfelt knowledge of one's impact.

PATH OF CHANGE

The Path of Change requires you to examine:

- How *adaptable* you are receiving *feedback* from associates.
- How often you seek *feedback* to help improve your *adaptability*.

Adaptability

Ask yourself these questions:

1. Am I willing to put aside my own interests for the sake of the organization?
2. Do I adjust my schedule to accommodate others' needs whenever this is required?
3. Even though I push myself hard, am I respectful of my own limits?
4. Even though I push others hard, am I respectful of their limits?
5. Am I willing to look at and admit my own mistakes?
6. Do I thrive on change more than I fear it?
7. Do I know that the qualities that have made me successful in the past may no longer serve me in the future?
8. Is it easy for me to fight stagnation and inertia?
9. Am I willing to change myself based on the feedback I receive from others?

Why is adaptability so important to knowing your impact? How does adaptability relate to each of the other capacities? Record in your journal how adaptability affects or is affected by each of the following:

- Interaction with associates (e.g., are you adaptable when you interact?)
- Understanding your contribution (e.g., if you are adaptable, do you contribute more or less?)
- Seeing positive intentions (e.g., does being adaptable lead to making positive attributions?)
- Stopping to reflect (e.g., does reflection increase or decrease adaptability?)
- Working through actions (e.g., how does working through actions increase adaptability?)
- Empathy (e.g., is empathy the result or cause of adaptability?)

After you have reflected on these, rank the above capacities from 1–6, one being your strongest and six being the one that requires the most work.

Feedback

This is the most straightforward of all the capacities. All that is required is that you ask an associate or coach to review your list with you and give you his or her honest opinion.

Chapter 7

Associates Have a Choice: They Ultimately Will Go Along or Not (Humility and Humbleness)

> *How does the sea become the king of all rivers*
> *and streams? Because it lies lower than them.*
> —Lao Tzu, *Chinese poet and philosopher*

Let's not forget that our associates always have a choice. They will decide whether or not they will allow you to lead them. They will decide whether they respect you enough to listen to you. They will decide whether they trust you. They will decide whether or not they will get on board with you.

Think back to the various principles and virtues that we have discussed so far. We outlined the difference among management, leadership and heart-centered leadership. We discussed the power of "knowing thyself." We addressed the importance of not judging people—or assuming you know why someone is saying or doing something—but opening your heart and your mind and coming to understand. We presented the concept of being more authentic and understanding that we all are basically the same—we want to know the truth. Your associates need what you need. In the last chapter, we discussed your impact. Through all of these chapters, we hope we have conveyed that these principles are not easy to live by. As we write, both of us feel that much of what we have to say may seem overly idealistic and not relevant. The key lies in your recognition that, no matter what you say and do, you must understand that your associates hold the key. They will make the choice to follow you or not. In fact, you can practice all the principles we have outlined, but if you do so without humility, you will likely fail. It is no wonder that humility is seen as the root of all virtues. As they say, "Pride goeth before destruction, and an haughty spirit before a fall."[1]

Countering Cynicism with Humbleness and Humility

In preparing this book, we presented our ideas to a class of undergraduate business majors. We received mixed reactions that were somewhat humbling. Some students resonated with the message of heart-centered leadership but said, "Be realistic—this stuff won't make it in the dog-eat-dog world out there." Other students believed that the message was important and were themselves struggling with how to lead a more ethical life as they considered careers in business. We

> Humility, that low, sweet root,
> from which all heavenly virtues shoot.
> —Thomas Moore,
> 19th-century Irish poet and musician
>
> Humility is the solid
> foundation of all the virtues.
> —Confucius, ancient Chinese sage

presented our ideas shortly after the Enron debacle, in which a huge company went bankrupt, and—partly because of questionable work practices—tens of thousands of investors were reportedly defrauded out of billions of dollars. Needless to say, the students were somewhat disillusioned with any talk about leadership and idealism.

Whether it is cautiousness, cynicism or just a good sense of reality, we thought these students had their wits about them. At different points as we wrote this book, we embraced the devilish possibility that there are just too many barriers to enact the principles of heart-centered leadership. It is not easy, it requires strong character and moral fiber, and the payoff is unsure. As the students pointed out, the real world does not always reward the heart-centered leader. Who has the time and energy to develop these qualities? Perhaps what we have to say is mere philosophy that has no ground with checks and balances or standard operating procedures. Moreover, many corrupt leaders have appealed to higher principles and ideals while causing great suffering.

We have three responses to these concerns: (1) heart-centered leadership works, (2) it's not idealistic and (3) you have to stay humble. First, we believe that, in the long run, heart-centered leadership works. In Chapter 1, we briefly reviewed some of the research on the effectiveness of leaders who possess the traits we describe. And there are financial benefits to practicing heart-centered principles.

> *The purpose of a business firm is not simply to make a profit, but it is to be found in its very existence as a community of persons who in various ways are endeavoring to satisfy their basic needs and who form a particular group at the service of the whole of society. Profit is a regulator of the life of a business, but it is not the only one; other human and moral factors must also be considered, which in the long term are at least equally important for the life of a business.*
> —*Pope John Paul II in* The Hundredth Year: An Essay

You may think that the gist of this quote lies in the words *profit, community, service, human* and *moral.* We also wish to emphasize the key phrase *in the long term.* We do not promise success overnight. Indeed, your image of success may transform as you practice the principles in this book. But heart-centered leadership, as we have tried to show, takes time, patience and perseverance.

Second, when we talk about heart-centered leadership, we are not saying that leaders should be soft, caring, nurturing, philanthropic or merely democratic. In serving the whole and putting their own desires behind those of the greatest good, leaders must sometimes be unpopular, give orders and go against the common will.

> *All leaders or bosses should be able to pay attention to the objective requirements of the situation without fussing too much about the delicate sensitivity of the followers or of the employees, of the people who have to take orders—the kind of person who must be loved by all will not make a good leader in most situations. The leader must be able to say 'no,' to be decisive, to be strong enough to do battle, if that is objectively necessary, to be tough, to fire, to hurt people, to give pain, etc. Or to put it another way, the boss in most situations cannot afford to be what we call weak— or ruled by fear. He or she must be courageous enough for the situation.*[2]
> —*from* Maslow on Management

When we talked about "open-mindedness" (Chapter 3), we were not advocating idealistic naiveté. Nor does "they need what you need" (Chapter 4) refer to making everyone happy. We also urged you to "let go" (Chapter 5)—to temper any egoistic desire to get your way—and consider the bigger picture. "Letting go" doesn't mean letting everybody walk all over you. Heart-centered leadership is about attending to reality—the "objective requirements of the situation"—but with integrity and detachment, in an open-minded and authentic manner.

Finally, it's also about attending to these requirements with humbleness and humility. As we listened to the students, we felt that their cautiousness, cynicism and reality concerns were based on the overwhelming feelings that accompany putting these principles into action. It is a humbling task. When we realize that heart-centered leadership is not easy, we have a simple choice to make. We can give up and succumb to the belief we live in a dog-eat-dog world, or we can be deeply humbled by the task that awaits us. Humility and cynicism are two sides of the same coin. You can prepare your heart to embrace the fact that others may not go along with you, or you can harden yourself and let the world of business take over your spirit.

We believe that the world is what we make it. As leaders, we are humbled by the recurrent awareness that success requires willing followers. While heart-centered leadership may seem lofty, you can't lead without willing followers. If you impulsively forge ahead and try to make things happen the way you want them to, without paying attention to the will of your associates, you will most likely be in for a rough ride. You might as well learn something about humility. You can let the world bring you to your knees, or you can strive to understand your role as a strong servant.

They Have a Choice

This chapter addresses the need for humility and humbleness. As leaders, we don't express these virtues often enough. We find ourselves thinking that our associates should feel grateful to have a good job for which they are well compensated, and they should be more appreciative of the opportunity to work with us and our organization. Although we agree humbleness should be extended on the part of both leader and associate, let's not forget that our associates have a choice. They decide whether they will allow you to lead them. They decide whether they respect you enough to listen to you. They decide whether they trust you. They decide whether they will get on board with you.

Associates love or leave their work for any given number of reasons. A great deal of research has been conducted to determine how organizations can increase their retention rates. Here are a few questions to ask yourself:

- How important do your associates feel in their work?
- What have you done as a leader to show them their importance?
- When was the last time you made it possible for your associates to be proud of their work?
- How often do you celebrate success?
- What are you doing to make work satisfying, rewarding and interesting?

These questions address the deeper attitudes of your associates, not just their actions and behaviors. There is a wide gulf between an associate's behavioral compliance with a request and his or her inner commitment to what he or she is doing. There is a good deal of research in social psychology on coercive persuasion and attitude change. People who feel required or expected to espouse attitudes may do so in behavior, but internally they are not committed. In other words, the attitude is not stable, and it can change after people leave the external situation.

Think about it. Have you ever worked in a situation where you went along with the status quo just to keep your job, to please a boss or to get a raise? As a leader, the more you try to coerce, demand or shove an idea down your associates' throats, the more they will resist you. They may say or act differently, but inside they don't buy it. So part of being humble means you must also be teachable. You have to be willing to admit your mistakes, and accept that your associates have a choice. Heart-centered means you cannot simply demand compliance.

Phil Evans, president of ProtoCall™ Services Inc., is teachable. ProtoCall provides 24-hour telephone intake, assessment and crisis counseling services to more than 100 different organizations who deliver behavioral health, community services, work-life and employee assistance programs. ProtoCall handles 35,000 confidential calls a month, many of which can be life-changing or even lifesaving when a suicidal client calls in. This is serious, heart-centered work, and Phil wants everyone to understand how important this work is. He also knows employees have a choice. In our interview, he revealed how humility and knowing your impact (see Chapter 6) go hand in hand:

> *I went head to head with someone who felt that they shouldn't have to show up to work on time. Or at least that's how I chose to interpret his behavior. So I reacted poorly and really screwed things up. "You need to get here on time!" "We run a serious business and take calls that could be a matter of life or death!" The employee responded with claims about unfair treatment, called in an attorney, said I singled him out. I stayed angry a long time about his sense of entitlement. I did not know how to talk to him with my heart. I did not know how to listen. It became a power struggle.*
>
> *There is no heart in a power struggle. I think a quote from the* Tao Te Ching, *sums it up:*
>
> > *'Control over others is strength, control over oneself is power.'*
>
> *I have come to realize that I have to watch myself and bring care to my words and actions. I have a great deal of responsibility over the potential impact and power of my words on others. Because I am really here to serve, I continue to be humbled by the people who work here. Now I know I could have simply used a different, gentler approach and have avoided the whole mess. When something*

doesn't go right, it is simply a problem to be addressed. It is not 'Uh-oh! Phil is going to be pissed off!' Rather, it is, 'What do we need to do together to correct this situation?' We work together toward certain principles.

From this and other incidents Phil has learned that "every leader has to be led." In recognizing associates have a choice, he now "chunks issues up to higher principles" when talking with them. Instead of focusing on what they are *not* doing, or trying to get them to change, he asks about the principles behind actions. "Do you believe this is important work?" "Do you believe that we have to be accountable to those who need our services?" "Do we need to behave in ways that show that accountability?" And he supports, acknowledges and reinforces associates as they hold to the higher standards—the principles—they themselves espouse.

Practicing Vision Statements in Challenging Times
To ensure high morale, Radio Shack adopted this simple five-principle creed:

1. All people are good.
2. People, workers, management and the company are all the same thing.
3. Every single person in the company must understand the essence of the business.
4. Every employee must benefit from the company's success.
5. You must create an environment where all of the above can happen.

We think this five-point creed speaks volumes for a company's values, and we have seen a number of similar mission statements, guiding principles and vision statements. The problem is that these are rarely put into action. They look great on the wall, but living these principles is the moment of truth, especially when the organization is faced with difficult times. It is easy to lead during good times. We are well compensated and trusted to lead during tough times. These vision and mission statements, like the guiding principles of heart-centered leadership, are to be used and lived every day if you want associates to follow you.

The World Trade Center attack on September 11, 2001, initiated a period that will be recorded in U.S. history as tremendously challenging for organizations and people around the world. The travel industry was hit the hardest. Southwest Airlines—well known and respected in the industry for exemplary financial performance—was one of the few airlines that chose to stay firm to its principles and did not lay off any employees during that time. We were curious to discover whether Southwest would stick to its convictions during this time—and it did.

We talked with a mechanic who worked for Southwest and asked him why Southwest didn't lay off staff during this time. He said, "Southwest would park a plane before they would lay an employee off." You must understand what a significant statement that is. First, in the airline industry, parking a plane represents a tremendous loss of revenue. Second, this associate had deeply internalized his belief in the culture of this organization. He really understood the company's principles. These principles did not just appear on a fancy poster in the hallway of the company's headquarters—you simply can't buy loyalty like that. The vision, mission and guiding principles are supposed to be the lighthouse for the organization. They should guide you through good and hard times.

Practicing Humility

Supervisors should remember how difficult and time-consuming even the simplest of tasks seemed the first time through. Be modest about your achievements and try not to inform your staff about how smart you are. Your firm can and will be able to survive without your services some day. Your staff needs you to help them grow professionally instead of listening to your autobiography.[3]

How do you get from a mission statement or a good set of principles (like those of Radio Shack) to the kind of loyalty shown by the mechanic at Southwest? The answer lies in your willingness and ability to be supportive, to show that you are there to get the work done, to provide assistance whenever it is needed or to lend a hand because you believe in the organization and people who work there. It also depends on your willingness to let your associates teach you, surprise you and help you. Below is a great story that illustrates this from *Speaker's Sourcebook II* by Glen Vanekeren.

I went on a search to become a leader.

I searched high and low. I spoke with authority. People listened. But alas, there was one who was wiser than I, and they followed that individual.

I sought to inspire confidence, but the crowd responded, "Why should I trust you?"

I postured, and I assumed the look of leadership with a countenance that flowed with confidence and pride. But many passed me by and never noticed my air of elegance.

I ran ahead of the others, pointed the way to new heights. I demonstrated that I knew the route to greatness. And then I looked back, and I was alone.

"What shall I do?" I queried. "I've tried hard and used all that I know." And I sat down and pondered long.

And then, I listened to the voices around me. And I heard what the group was trying to accomplish. I rolled up my sleeves and joined in the work.

As we worked, I asked, "Are we all together in what we want to do and how to get the job done?"

And we thought together, and we fought together, and we struggled towards our goal.

I found myself encouraging the fainthearted. I sought the ideas of those too shy to speak out. I taught those who had little skill. I praised those who worked hard. When our task was completed, one of the group turned to me and said, "This would not have been done but for your leadership."

At first, I said, "I didn't lead. I just worked with the rest." And then I understood, leadership is not a goal. It's a way of reaching a goal.

I lead best when I help others to go where we've decided to go. I lead best when I help others to use themselves creatively. I lead best when I forget about myself as leader and focus on my group ... their needs and their goals.
To lead is to serve ... to give ... to achieve together.[4]

So ask yourself these questions. Have you earned your associates' respect? Have you earned their trust? Would you follow a leader like yourself? We understand how difficult the role of the leader can be. It is a daunting and complicated path. As we stated in the very beginning of this book, we are all human and therefore imperfect. We have made every mistake a leader can make, and hopefully we have learned a great deal from those experiences and are better leaders today. Yet we also know that in some cases, on some days, we have probably not learned the lessons well.

Listening

Over the years, we have asked associates to tell us what they want and need from their leaders. What would it take to follow their leaders without hesitation? Listed below are some of their thoughts:[5]

- I would like my manager to walk in my shoes; to really understand what I go through day in and day out; and how greatly the decisions he or she makes affect me.
- Sometimes I feel I am viewed only as a number, but, like all people, I am human. I have love and fear in my life, but I am also filled with hope and frustrations.
- I would appreciate being told the truth—the good, the bad and the ugly.
- I just want to be appreciated, listened to and understood.
- Before you make any major decisions that affect my work, could you please include me in the thought process? After all, I am

closer to the work and could probably show you how to make it work.

> Since in order to speak, one must first listen, learn to speak by listening.
> —Rumi, Sufi poet[6]
>
> The greatest truths are the simplest, and so are the greatest men.
> —J. C. Hare[7]

- I will probably accept almost any change if you would tell me why we're doing it.
- Please understand that I am surviving life. I am raising a family. I pay taxes and manage a home. I make important decisions every day. Please give me credit for having a brain. I can participate in the decision-making process.
- I often hear leaders ask the question, "How do I motivate my staff?" Here's a clue—stop trying to! Instead, just be you, just be authentic, just share who you are and I will be motivated.
- To be really successful, understand that we need each other for success. I need you as much as you need me.
- I wish that general managers, regional managers and on up would show more concern for department heads and staff. More often than not, I've been turned away by my general manager because she's "too busy" or "has a phone call coming." Our regional manager keeps canceling property visits, so we can't even discuss our needs with anyone. I wish this company would just go back to being itself, instead of trying to be so important.

As you can see from these comments, these associates aren't asking for much. In fact, the message here is quite simple and resonates with the virtue of humility. They really want us to do what is right—be authentic, real and lead in a heart-centered way.

Exercise

There has been some research on humility that suggests it is comprised of the following six components.[8] Under each of the components, we have listed several questions for you to consider. Write your answers to these questions in your journal.

1. Accurate assessment of one's abilities and achievements (not unduly favorable or unfavorable)
   - Do you have a tendency to boast about your achievements?
   - Do you have a tendency to downplay or minimize your achievements?
   - In a job interview, do you give an accurate picture of your skills and abilities?
   - Have you ever been told that you misrepresented yourself?

2. Ability to acknowledge one's mistakes, imperfections, gaps in knowledge and limitations
   - Do you openly acknowledge your mistakes and limitations to your associates?
   - Would you tell an associate that you cannot perform a certain task?
   - Would you consider yourself to be a perfectionist?
   - Do you have difficulty admitting you don't know something?

3. Openness to new ideas, contradictory information and advice
   - Do you have to be the one who brings the new idea to the table?
   - If an associate contradicts you, what is your knee-jerk reaction?
   - How often do you sincerely ask for advice from associates?
   - Are you willing to seek out others to get a fresh perspective on things?

4. Keeping of one's abilities and accomplishments—one's place in the world—in perspective
   - Do you tend to see yourself as the most important one at work?
   - Do you feel there is more to be learned or that you have accomplished all you need to know?
   - How often do you reflect on the fact that your position or business might be able to continue without you?
   - How often do you consider that you were not always in the position you are in today?

5. Relatively low self-focus, a "forgetting of the self"
   - Do you spend a lot of time focusing on how you are doing or performing?
   - Are you anxious to know whether others consider your ideas, opinions and general "works" important?
   - How much time during the workday do you really focus on taking care of others and the business versus trying to excel, lead or perform?
   - After work, to what do you devote your attention?

6. Appreciate the value, as well as the many different ways that people and things can contribute to our world
   - How often do you feel appreciation or gratitude for the contributions of your associates?
   - Where do you consider the value of your business to lie? In your associates? Your products? Your suppliers? Your customers? All of these?
   - When you encounter obstacles (e.g., policies, budget problems, procedural flaws), is your tendency to react or to take a bigger perspective?
   - Would your associates see you as appreciating many aspects of work? Different people? Or just some aspects and some people?

Chapter 8
Care for the Heart (Self-Care/Emotional Health)

Every now and then go away, have a little relaxation,
for when you come back to your work your judgment will be surer.
—Leonardo da Vinci

Do not worry; eat three square meals a day; say your prayers; be courteous to your creditors;
keep your digestion good; exercise; go slow and easy. Maybe there are other things your special case
requires to make you happy, but, my friend, these I reckon will give you a good lift.
—Abraham Lincoln

In this chapter, we discuss the importance of health, balance and self-care. Each of the preceding heart-centered principles will strengthen when you take care of your heart—that is, when you commit to practices for physical, social, spiritual and emotional well-being. There is a wealth of methods and strategies that leaders can use to improve their own heart health and the health of their work environment. We review some of these in the chapter. More importantly, we want to convey just how important the organ we call the heart is to effective leadership. We are amazed by the number of stories of heart attacks and physical and nervous breakdowns among managers, leaders and executives when they do not practice heart-centered principles.

Self-care for the heart is so critical to heart-centered leadership that we want to provide you with many points of access for understanding and nurturing your heart. We also want to explore what the heart actually is. Research tells us that the heart is not just a physical organ or pump. This chapter reviews recent breakthroughs and scientific understandings about the heart to help you decide how best to care for your heart. We also review several philosophical or spiritual meanings about the heart because we believe that meaning, fulfillment, spirituality or a sense of wonder is part of caring for the heart.

Stories About (Not) Caring for the Heart

There are many stories—new and old—of leaders who either failed to practice heart-centered principles or whose workaholism or greed cost them their health and happiness. John D. Rockefeller (1839-1937), once one of the richest men in the world, is reported by his biographers to have been cold, ruthless, cunning, shrewd and hated by many businessmen because he brought them ruin. These business practices made him rich, but around the age of 50, they also led to a physical and nervous breakdown. He was frightened by this breakdown, went into semiretirement, and made health and longevity important personal goals. Rockefeller changed his lifestyle in several ways that included a good diet, adequate rest and plenty of exercise. Equally important, he made it a point not to worry.

He also made social health, his own and others, a priority. First, instead of thinking only about *getting* money, he thought about how he could help others and began *giving* millions away. This practice continues today through the Rockefeller Foundation, which Rockefeller established "to promote the well-being of mankind throughout the world." In 2000, the foundation gave away $200 million. Second, Rockefeller used golf as his own personal form of exercise. But golf was not only about physical exercise. Rockefeller did not allow fellow golfers to discuss business, but used the opportunity for lighthearted and enjoyable conversation. One of his biographers reports:

> *During the heyday of the antitrust trial against Standard Oil, Rockefeller was seen as an ogre and a curmudgeon. In fact, he was a pretty genial character with a good sense of humor and a very social life. Usually, he would be out on the golf course with eight, 10 people, who would then be invited to lunch. I was struck in my research that this man was always with other people, when his image was that of a brooding loner.*[1]

The story of Rockefeller—a driven, almost heartless competitor who was transformed into a more caring, heart-centered leader—repeats itself in hundreds, if not thousands, of executives every year. The turning point is often a crisis in health, whether physical (such as heart attack, stress disorder) or social (divorce, estrangement). John D. Rockefeller died at the ripe old age of 98.

Cases of executives' heart problems or heart failure reveal how important care for the heart is to the bottom line. The connection between a leader's health and financial performance can be dramatic. Roberto Goizueta—one-time Coca-Cola CEO and chain-smoker—had serious health problems, and Coca-Cola's stock declined after his death from cancer in 1997. Jerry Junkins, CEO of Texas Instruments, suffered a fatal heart attack in 1996; the company's stock price fell 25 percent within weeks.

But, for every one of these dramatic examples, there are many others that show how executives can do something to intervene or prevent problems. Sometimes interventions are costly, but worthwhile. In 1994, Michael Eisner of Disney underwent quadruple bypass surgery, and Disney stock prices dropped; however, Eisner's return brought a surge in stock prices. Interventions can be prudent. Jack Welch, former CEO of General Electric, underwent angioplasty and bypass surgery in 1995, and stock prices actually improved.

Recovery from heart failure can inspire a new type of leadership. Dave Marsing, a plant manager at Intel Corporation's largest plant, had a heart attack in 1990 at age 36, when Intel was having difficulty producing the "chip of the future." Marsing's story of recovery is about his commitment to Intel, and to creating a work environment where balance and compassion exist. On a personal level, Marsing uses meditation, exercise and a balanced work schedule. At work, he believes in keeping his associates happy: "If the goal is to maximize profits, then it seems obvious to me that the best way to get there is to have happy people who are motivated to work ... Imagine if you could build a company that was capable of learning from all its experiences, as well as from other companies' experiences. What you'd get is a new kind of asset: corporate wisdom. Now, combine that with the kind of compassion that accepts employees for who they really are, that motivates them to reach their potential, and you'd have something truly extraordinary."[2]

Care for the Heart (Self-Care/Emotional Health)

Each of these stories reveals that the heart plays a critical role in leadership transformation. Why is it so powerful? What, in fact, is this physical organ we call the heart?

What Is the Heart?

Choose one or more of the descriptions below.

a) The organ that pumps the blood for circulation throughout the human body.

b) The organ that synthesizes and synchronizes information from all over the body and brings an internal sense of consistency, order or coherence to the body and mind.

c) The center of the soul or inner self.

d) The organ that contains memories of each person's cells.

Although response (a) is the most commonly understood or most "scientific," there is increasing evidence that other definitions are legitimate. We refer to the research of Dean Ornish, M.D.[3]; Candace Pert, M.D.[4]; Paul Pearsall, M.D.[5]; as well as to Rollin McCraty, M.D.[6], and his colleagues at the Institute of HeartMath®. This science—still in its early stages—indicates the heart is a grand communicator or integrator. Integration occurs not only through the blood, but also through connections to the brain and central nervous system, the immune system and all other body systems. The heart is sending information through neuropeptides, nutrients, energy, bioelectricity, rhythm, cycles, vibration and magnetic fields. The heart is at the center of the body-mind interface. These findings should send a signal to aspiring managers and leaders. Taking care of the heart is not only about caring for your "pump," but also about staying in touch with your own capacity to circulate, communicate and integrate. Of course, we need to eat well and avoid certain foods so that we don't clog the heart. But optimal heart health involves more than diet. It's about a balanced lifestyle, spending time with loved ones, emotional intelligence and taking time out for reflection.

Evidence that the heart has memory is revealed in research and stories about heart transplant recipients. Researchers observed psychological changes in the recipients that paralleled the experiences of their donors. Parallels included preferences related to changes in food, music, art, sex, recreation and careers, as well as specific instances of perceptions of names and sensory experiences related to the donors (e.g., one donor was killed by a gunshot to the face; the recipient had dreams of seeing hot flashes of light in his face).[7]

Of course, scientific evidence for the soul is harder to prove. However, around the world and in most cultures, when people are asked to point to the location of their "self," they are much more likely to point to the upper chest, or to the region surrounding their hearts, than to their heads, pelvises, gut areas, or any other part of their bodies. We may instinctively know that this is the origin of our being. Scientists have known that the heart of a fetus beats long before the brain begins forming. And for centuries, poets and writers have referred to the heart as the seat of the soul or self. When we fall in love, it would be ridiculous to say, "I give you my brain," but romantic and appropriate to say, "I give you my heart."

Whether or not the heart is more than a pump, the seat of the soul, or the vessel of cellular memories, we do know that it is a vulnerable organ, especially when people lack social support and love in their lives. Dean Ornish, in his book *Love and Survival*,[8] reviewed an abundance of scientific studies from social support literature. These studies strongly suggest individuals live longer, have fewer instances of heart disease, and are more likely to recover from cardiovascular problems (stroke, heart attack) if they have family or a social network which cares about them. There is a strong relationship between intimacy and the health of one's heart. However, there is no single explanation for this connection.

Executive Health and Performance

So, we know that executives who don't take care of their hearts may cause problems for themselves as well as their companies. And it seems that the heart holds a lot of wisdom. But, many hard-working managers or aspiring leaders say: "So what? I have to make compromises. To get ahead, I sometimes have to work hard, sleep less and eat on the run. Let me get further ahead in my career. I'll take care of myself later!" You may be such a person. Here are some pointers if self-care is not your thing.

In fact, self-care is strongly related to the other principles. First, remember the principle *"know thyself"*? It is important to *know* the special risks that ambitious leaders and executives face. Second, optimal performance depends on leaders exercising some moderation in lifestyle. We hope you'll be *open-minded* and hear us out on the importance of leaders' health. Third, remember the principle *"know your impact"* from Chapter 6? You set an important example for your associates if you don't take good care of yourself. In our work doing 360-degree assessments with associates, we find them concerned that their leaders do not have work-life balance. More importantly, you will run into serious health care costs and raise company insurance rates if, as a whole, you have an unhealthy associate population.

A Special Risk for Executives. According to top researchers in the field of executive health, business leaders have a special set of self-care risks.[9] These include physical demands which prevent them from taking breaks for exercise and rest (extensive travel, time pressures, long hours), as well as psychological demands (loneliness of command, decision-making pressures, many transitions). Often, executives have an Achilles' heel, or predisposition toward poor health, that can be recognized and managed. For example, because of genetics, some of us are more prone to cardiovascular disorder, cancer or depression. Each of these problems can be managed through effective risk assessment and lifestyle management. However, some executives ignore the results of their annual medical exams or discount single problems. Alternatively, they may neglect physical exercise and eat poorly during the work week.

Given the highly complex and integrative nature of leadership, it is no wonder that cardiovascular disease is one of the greatest health risks for executives. This is why caring for the heart is so important. Such care will help prevent heart disease and also provide the psychological foundation and physical resources—the resting place—that enable leaders to perform the high-level integration and communication tasks required of them. This is why executive health goes beyond physical care and encompasses psychological, spiritual and ethical dimensions of health. Executive health requires such abilities as the capacity to love, to reach out for support and share worries and concerns; and the moral strength to make the right decisions under financial pressure.

> *Spiritually alive executives recognize that there is more to life than the immediate positions they are in. They are aware of a greater objective to life. Having a more global view to their personal lives, spiritually whole executives can move beyond themselves to embrace the needs and desires of others. They can recognize their ability to go beyond the basic functions of the organization, using their positions and power to enhance the lives of the organization's members and the community as a whole.*[10]

Manager Health Makes a Difference. Over the past decade, the American Psychological Association and the National Institutes of Health have co-sponsored several international scientific conferences on work, stress and health. We have attended these conferences and listened to researchers from all over the world talk about the negative impact of work on health and ways of improving the health status of associates. Over and over again, scientists report the same finding: one of the best predictors of associates' health and well-being is their own perception that they have direct supervisors who themselves are healthy, and who provide genuine support and encouragement. In other words, having a supportive and caring supervisor seems to contribute to associate health and buffer against the normal stressors of the work day. Alternatively, having an angry,

What You Can Do: Health Promotion Works!

Taking care of your health and taking care of your employees' health are money-making propositions. Research suggests that for every dollar you invest in wellness and health promotion efforts for your associates, you will receive a return on investment of nearly $6. These efforts include classes and programs in cardiovascular disease prevention, as well as smoking cessation, physical fitness, health risk appraisals, nutrition, stress management, high blood pressure control, prenatal care and weight management. There are some very helpful organizations that can guide and support you in designing an effective wellness program for your organization:

- Wellness Councils of America (www.welcoa.org)
- The National Wellness Institute (www.nationalwellness.org)
- The American College of Environmental and Occupational Medicine; see especially the Corporate Health Achievement Award (www.chaa.org)
- The National Institute of Occupational Safety & Health (NIOSH) (www.cdc.gov/niosh/homepage.html)

To learn more about the financial benefits of health promotion, see Chapman, Larry S., 2003. "Meta-evaluation of worksite health promotion: Economic return studies." *American Journal of Health Promotion/The Art of Health Promotion* 17, 3 (January/February): 1-9.

unsympathetic or unavailable supervisor only adds to associate stress and health problems.

For example, research indicates that a supervisor's level of self-care and heartfelt attitude affects the work performance of associates. One study of about 50 supervisors assessed the level of "Type-A," stress-prone personality (hard-driving, impatient, irritable) and a trait called negative affectivity (e.g., tendency toward anger, negativity and focus on the negative aspects of others).[11] The researchers found that Type-A supervisors had work units that performed well, but whose associates were more likely to be unhealthy, report depression and show chronic irritability. Negative supervisors had work units that performed less well. These and other findings suggest that hard-driving leadership qualities may result in short-term achievements, but at the expense of associate health.

Another study of 50 managers found strong relationships among biological measures of heart health and perceptions of the work environment. Managers' cholesterol levels were lower when they perceived social support both at and away from work. Their cholesterol levels were higher when they perceived hassles and bad communication at work, and especially when the work environment was described as bureaucratic— that is, where rules and regulations were preferred over the initiative of associates. This study suggests that managers themselves are less likely to be healthy when they feel constrained.[12]

These and other studies suggest a strong feedback loop among leader health, work environment and associate health. Higher-up executives set a tone and pace that trickles down. It is important to know your impact in the area of health, as well as in terms of management style, performance and operational savvy. A healthy work climate creates a sense of participation, loyalty, vitality and psychological presence among associates.

Setting the Example. Skills for effective leadership to create healthy work environments have been discussed by various authors and researchers. We refer here to the work of Robert Rosen, Judd Allen, Cary Cooper, Jim

Quick and others. In synthesizing the work of these authors, we see that heart-centered leadership requires the broad skill of continuously tuning in and responding to health feedback from associates and the work climate. This broad skill can be broken into various components (see Figure 8.1 on the next page).

- Your own level of health is the most important factor, for it allows you to set, calibrate, or modulate the pace or pressure of the work climate. Recall the study of the hard-driving Type-A managers. They got a lot done, but at the cost of wearing down associates. Again, know how your own pace impacts the work climate.

- Your own health serves as a model of wellness lifestyle to your associates and sends a strong message about what is the appropriate level of work, rest, recreation and socialization. You also model acceptable practices for stress relief. Think about the difference between drinking heavily at company parties and joining in a jog during lunch. If you are healthy, you are also more available to provide support to others.

- Two key principles from earlier chapters have a core idea. "They need what you need" and "don't judge but come to understand" require paying attention to associates, seeing things from their perspective and understanding their problems. Most organizations deal with at least one of several key, health-related problems such as: sick leave, excessive absenteeism, inadequate benefits packages, workers' compensation, alcohol or drug abuse, violence and sexual harassment. An increasing number of associates report problems with depression and anxiety. When problems like these arise, you have a choice. On one hand, you can tolerate, minimize, ignore or rationalize the problem. Alternatively, you can search for ways to be more responsive, whether that response is empathetic, concerned, coaching, disciplinary or a mixture. Sometimes, all that is needed is a show of concern and support to those partners who can facilitate responsiveness in your absence. This may be human resource personnel, safety directors and any affiliates that provide support to associates (e.g., employee assistance programs; wellness-program personnel). When you ignore problems, you send a strong message, and problems swept under the rug can surface as crises later.

- Just as you monitor and respond to individual associates, you can also monitor the work climate through surveys, focus groups and town meetings. There are a number of survey instruments available to tap into the level of health in the work climate. Just make sure when you collect data you provide clear, useful and specific feedback.

Paths to Caring for the Heart

There are many paths to caring for the heart. Your heart has its own unique pattern of beating, pumping, and circulating chemicals and energy throughout your body. It also has its own electromagnetic signature of pulsation that tunes into or resonates with different frequencies in others' hearts and the world around you. More and more, research suggests that cardiovascular health depends on a holistic and balanced lifestyle that brings together many different paths to caring for the heart. These include: exercise, diet and relaxation; stress, time and energy management; avoidance of addictive habits (substance abuse, excessive eating or gambling, sex, etc.); spiritual or contemplative exercises (meditation or prayer); having fun; listening to relaxing, uplifting or energizing music; enjoying a good laugh; taking regular vacations; taking time away from work regularly and—perhaps most important of all—having social support and being with people about

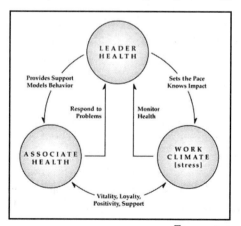

Figure 8.1

whom you care, and who care about you. It may sound trite, but having love in your life is a great way of caring for your heart. Indeed, a key predictor of heart attacks is the presence of hostility, repressed anger and unresolved resentments.

As we have said elsewhere, heart-centered leadership is not easy. We would be remiss if we didn't remind you to take it easy and go slowly as you learn to practice the principles and virtues outlined in previous chapters. We also would be negligent if we didn't encourage you to continually take care of yourself on the journey of heart-centered leadership. You must have a stopping or resting place. You must find a way to tune into your internal rhythms. You must be able to admit your vulnerability and not push yourself too hard. You must find your own unique routine and strategy for taking care of your heart. Finally, you must give yourself permission to make a few mistakes along the way.

We think that practicing the previous six principles will be good for your heart. Being open-minded, humble, trusting—each of these is about practicing good human relationship principles. When we treat others as we wish to be treated, we generally experience less stress. However, in addition to these principles, you also need a regimen for physical health. The two sets of practices—physical care for the heart and heart-centered leadership—strengthen each other in a win-win arrangement.

When you take care of your heart, however you do it, you are providing necessary support and nourishment that allow you to go out and work hard as a leader. Heart nourishment provides you the extra resources, and personal

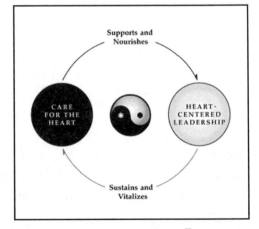

Figure 8.2

strength and power, to practice the principles in a real way. In our research on heart-centered leaders, we have noticed that they always have a strong sense of personal presence, wakefulness and "realness" about them. These are "hearty" folks.

Additionally, when you practice heart-centered principles, you are helping your blood flow and the energy of your heart move out in the world in real and vital ways that enrich the lives of others. Putting these human relations principles into practice makes you feel good, and helps sustain and vitalize your heart. It is exhilarating to make deeper connections with your associates, and see how you enrich the lives of others.

Strategies for Caring for the Heart

As discussed previously, research suggests that the heart is a grand communicator and integrator. These findings support the practice of "integrative medicine," which combines the best of conventional Western medicine with mind-body-spirit approaches to health. These include effective practices such as massage, meditation, biofeedback, yoga, aromatherapy, herbalism and acupuncture. In this section, we briefly review some of these conventional and alternative approaches to self-care, and provide a wide list of resources to suit your particular orientation. Because some readers want to do something immediately, we also include a number of popular self-help resources.

Knowing Your Cardiovascular Risk Factors. Medical research identifies several factors that increase the risk of heart disease. Based on this research, a number of risk-calculation devices have been developed and are available over the Internet.[13] A simple risk assessment profile is provided here to get you started. This simple measure does not diagnose whether you have a problem. However, if you answer "yes" to any of the questions below, we suggest that you contact a physician if you have not done so recently. If you answer "yes" to four or more questions, seriously consider starting or enhancing a health and wellness program. Again, consult your doctor.

1. Are you 10 pounds over the ideal weight for your age and height?
2. Is your blood pressure greater than 140/90?
3. Is your cholesterol greater than 200?
4. Do you eat fried food almost every day?
5. Do you smoke or chew tobacco?
6. Do you do some form of active exercise less than 30 minutes a week?
7. Does heart disease run in your family?

Women and Heart Disease. Women readers should be aware that heart disease is the number one cause of death for females. You can search the Center for Disease Control's Web site for information on various topics, one of which is cardiovascular disease in women. (To search, go to www.cdc.gov, click on "Health Topics A to Z," click on "Women's Health," and click on "Cardiovascular Health Program." Alternately, go to www.cdc.gov/cvh. Women typically believe that heart disease is a man's disease, and therefore, fail to perceive it as a serious health threat. They have less access to bypass surgery and angioplasty, and when women undergo these operations, they have higher mortality rates than men. Conversely, women seem to be able to reverse heart disease more easily than men when they make comprehensive lifestyle changes. Visit the "Sister to Sister—Everyone Has a Heart Foundation" Web site to learn more about the special efforts to promote awareness among women (www.sistertosister.org).

Heart-Centered and Holistic Therapies. There are vast and growing numbers of counseling and meditative therapies that focus on healing and helping the heart from an emotional and psychosocial perspective. These include music therapy, hypnotherapy, contemplative practices, bodywork, psychodrama and breathwork. There are too many to list here, but readers may wish to visit the Web sites for The Wellness Institute (www.wellnessinstitute.org), The Eupsychia Institute for Well-Being (www.eupsychia.com), The Omega Institute for Holistic Studies (www.eomega.org), and Esalen Institute (www.esalen.org). The

Mindfulness-Based Stress Reduction Clinic, developed by Jon Kabat-Zinn and researchers at the University of Massachusetts, is offered at various hospitals and by mental health professionals around the country (www.umassmed.edu/cfm). Some readers, skeptical of these alternative therapeutic approaches, may want to investigate any of a number of books that review some of the scientific evidence.[14] Because of growing interest in these therapies, the National Institutes of Health recently established the National Center for Complementary and Alternative Medicine to investigate the validity of various approaches (nccam.nih.gov).

Institute of HeartMath®. There are several alternative self-care approaches that deserve special mention because of their focus on the heart. One of these is the Institute of HeartMath (www.heartmath.org). HeartMath is a science-based, easy-to-use stress reduction system that emphasizes guided imagery, visualization with music and biofeedback techniques. For example, individuals are guided in self-reflection on their emotional states as they listen to positive music to generate states of calm. A key finding in HeartMath pertains to changes in heart rate. Apparently, when individuals are calm, relaxed and have a sense of inner peace, the heart and autonomic nervous systems show more order or coherence. Alternatively, negative emotions lead to increased disorder in the autonomic nervous system and the heart's rhythms, adversely affecting the rest of the body. Through biofeedback, it is possible to train individuals to create more coherent heart rhythms that correspond to positive emotional states and a healthy heart.

Dean Ornish. The work of Dean Ornish, M.D., lends evidence that it is possible to reverse heart disease. Dr. Ornish developed a program where individuals with heart disease who wish to avoid bypass surgery practice a regimen of a healthy vegetarian diet, regular exercise, meditation and communication. His research shows that dramatic changes in lifestyle can lead to lower cholesterol and improved health and well-being. Due to the documented success of his approach, more than 40 insurance companies cover the Ornish program in hospitals across the United States. You can learn more about the Ornish program by reading his books and visiting the Web site for Preventive Medicine Research Institute (www.pmri.org).

Meanings of the Heart

This last section briefly presents ideas about the various ordinary and spiritual meanings ascribed to the heart. We cover these meanings because it has been well-established that spiritual health is a key factor in having a healthy heart.[15] Notice how you refer to the heart in your ordinary language, as well as in the ways you think about its extraordinary or spiritual meanings. First, reflect on the ways we use the word *heart*,[16] and notice whether you use these particular phrases:

- "Have a heart" — Be merciful
- "Change of heart" — Change your mind
- "Know by heart" — Memorize something
- "Broken heart" — Lose love
- "Heartfelt" — Deeply felt
- "Have your heart in the right place" — Be kind
- "Cry your heart out" — Grieve
- "Heavy heart" — Sadness
- "Have your heart set on" — Want something badly
- "Heart-to-heart" — Sincere and frank discussion

The word *heart* shares roots with the word *hearth*; both have Latin origins in *cor*, which is seen in the word *cardio*, but is also found in words like *courteous, cordial, courage, encourage* and *accord*. All of these speak to the emotional world of relationships. Also, the word *core* refers to the deepest or innermost center. We suggest reading the above phrases and words aloud one at a time, taking a pause between each, and listening inwardly for the feelings and sensations produced. Afterwards, try these words for contrast: *coldhearted, hard-hearted, heartless, heartbroken, heartrending, heartsick, heartache.* If done slowly, this may give you a real sense of the importance of language and how it resonates with the heart.

There are many spiritual references to and meanings for the word *heart* within all major religions, as well as all mystical or meditative traditions.[17] Whatever your religious background, we encourage you to reflect on these meanings as well. The following list is not meant to be exhaustive or scholarly. We only wish to show how important the heart is to spiritual health. We apologize if we have not represented your faith, religious or spiritual orientation. We also believe that heart-centered leadership requires a deep respect for diversity. Understanding how others lead their spiritual lives can provide helpful support for the six previous heart-centered principles, so we encourage you to keep an open mind as you read through the various spiritual meanings of *heart*.

Old Testament/Judaism.[18] The Old Testament contains more than 700 references to the word *heart*. Many of these references talk about having love for God in one's heart. According to Jewish tradition, the heart is the throne of God's glory, and a basic message of the Old Testament is intimacy between the heart of the individual and the heart of God.

Christianity. In the New Testament, there are more than 200 references to the word *heart*. These references talk about being pure of heart, and in the Roman Catholic faith, there are many references to the sacred hearts of Jesus and Mary.

Islam. In Islam, especially within the Sufi or mystical tradition, there is great emphasis on heart purification, and the image of giving wings to the heart is used poetically. Perhaps the most widely known Sufi poet is Jalaluddin Rumi (1207-1273), whose words speak to the desire for experiencing the divine presence in the ordinary occasions of our lives.

Buddhism. There are many meanings of the *heart* throughout Buddhist literature. Purity of heart often refers to having great clarity in perception that transcends all attachment, and the idea that one can only see clearly with the heart.

> Knowing constancy, the mind is open. With an open mind, you will be openhearted. Being openhearted, you will act royally.[20]

Taoism.[19] A key aspect of Taosim is an understanding of the Tao, interpreted as the Great

Way or Path of Life. To follow the Tao, one must cultivate traits like simplicity, spontaneity, flexibility, joyfulness and presence. Lao Tzu, the father of Taoism, taught that all straining and striving are counterproductive.

Again, we provide this brief list of spiritual or religious references to the *heart* as a reminder that it is a key part of spiritual health. Some readers may best understand how to take care of the heart through scripture or spiritual poetry, whereas others may feel that exercise, diet and a healthy lifestyle are sufficient. We hope that—whatever path you choose—you find the time to take care of your heart in a way that adds to your health and your capacity to lead in a heart-centered way.

Summary

We wrote this chapter to provide a critical and needed balance in the leadership literature. Indeed, we think that the "missing piece" or "hidden gold" of effective leadership lies in self-care, lifestyle and personal health. We hope that one or more of the sections of this chapter helped either to motivate or enlighten you to find this missing piece or polish your hidden gold. We believe that by caring for your heart, you will add more zest, more zeal, more enthusiasm and more vitality to your work as a heart-centered leader. Indeed, people will see you as putting "your whole heart" into your work. And they will benefit from your example.

> The noblest joy of the enses, the holiest piece of the heart, the most resplendent luster of all good works derives from this: that the creature puts his or her heart wholly into what he or she does.[21]

Chapter 9
Toward an Integral Model of Leadership: Practice the Virtues

In our own work—aspiring to be heart-centered leaders—we must make the effort to apply the exercises and principles in this book. For example, we asked our team members to rate us using the feedback form at the end of Chapter 2, "Know Thyself." Six of our associates unanimously agreed that we need to have more faith in the project, team and the organization. While this was not a surprise, it made us realize we have more work to do in the area of showing faith in our associates and that we need to practice living the principle of letting go (Chapter 5).

In working with the principle of letting go, we see more clearly how successful this team and the project were in spite of our worry and fear. In retrospect, we are awed by the fantastic work of our team members. In a few months, they recruited many businesses and established relationships with key personnel, designed surveys, coordinated schedules, managed budgets, dealt with the departure of a team member, hired new associates, ordered and designed materials, delivered training programs and much more. We experienced a greater force at work—one that was beyond our own desires or will. In a real way, our letting go has opened our hearts to our team. It is not always this way. There is an ebb and flow, and sometimes we get along better than others. But we continually make the effort to come back to the principles.

Any attempt to summarize or integrate the principles of this book must start from a place of reflection on your own experience, and, hopefully, will result in your creative use of the ideas we have discussed. As in our experience, we encourage you to deeply, honestly and earnestly look at how you "work the principles" in your relationship with your associates: how you seek to know yourself, let go of control, seek feedback, be authentic or act with integrity. We strongly encourage you to let the principles inform your perspective on leadership, your health and your own career perspective. We believe that a true integration of heart-centered principles can come only through your own work, and by learning from your own mistakes.

Working Through

In the exercise section of Chapter 6, we discussed "working through your actions" when knowing your impact. Remember that heart-centered leadership is a path of reflection as well as a path of action and change. "Working through" is a core reflection practice which requires not only that you seek feedback, but that you also act on that feedback. You must follow up with your associates again and again. You must remain vigilant about not discounting them, being disconnected, living in your head and going back into fear. Working through is core to integrating the principles. In a very real way, heart-centered integration requires working through problems and letting go of your own ego.

The pursuit of power is often a disguise for the desire to gain self-esteem and feel valued by others. This egotistical drive for power is so great that, as leaders climb into greater positions of authority and gain more recognition, they may neglect their connection with people. As a result, they often cannot maintain their high-ranking positions because it requires more influence than domination, more leadership than management and more perspective-taking than willful action.

Wisdom is knowing what to do next; virtue is doing it.
—David Starr Jordan, American naturalist[1]

In other words, the path that has taken you to your current leadership position is often not the same path you now need to travel to create heart-centered leadership. Janet Hagberg, in her book Real Power[2], explains that several issues and concerns may resurface from time to time as we grow in leadership: low self-worth, possessiveness (protecting turf), unwillingness to be vulnerable and the belief that one always has to project a strong and hard persona. In order to integrate the heart-centered principles, you must work continually with the "barriers" within your own psyche that get in the way of the heart.

Your ability to keep changing as you work through your issues is really the heart of heart-centered leadership. It is also the true definition of vision in leadership. Normally we think about vision in terms of organization, knowing our goals, developing strategies to carry out and ultimately realize our vision. But from the perspective of heart-centered leadership, vision is much more mundane. Its significance is felt in the way we work though issues in our day-to-day relationships with our associates and in the way we take care of ourselves. Christy L. Beaudin is corporate director for quality improvement at PacifiCare Behavioral Health. Christy's tendency is to be direct and forthright in her communications, a style which has not always served her well under stressful situations with exacting deadlines:

> Virtue is like precious odors, most fragrant when they are incensed or crushed.
> —Francis Bacon[3]

Vision? People think about a vision statement as something lofty that must be adhered to. No, it is very simple. You have to see. There are times when leaders have to use corrective lenses. And, the correction is different for different leaders. For me, it has been about learning how to communicate with people who don't like direct communication. When you don't have time, you have to be direct. You have to set up the backdrop to empower people. Over time, you start to see people as having different needs. For me, I now actively check in with people separately from the team process (e-mail and telephone) because they need extra attention.

I had to learn how to deviate from my standard operating behaviors and pay attention to how I talked to people, and even the words I chose. Now when deadlines occur, I think people have a better appreciation where I am coming from. I sometimes have to work longer (extended hours) because I have chosen to use different types of communication. But is it positive, or does it produce stress? It is a balancing act that has really paid off in the long run. My areas have significantly less turnover. I believe this results from showing that I care and am willing to take risks that others at my level may not. In turn, this places less stress on me, and I have better self-care.

For Christy, working through was about her practicing and balancing the virtues of self-care, foresight and authenticity. It was about really practicing vision, putting on corrective lenses, rather than remembering some abstract vision statement.

Concluding Note

We hope this book provides you with the means for working through your experiences as a leader. In the end, it is your own experience that will inform you as to whether a certain principle or virtue works at any given time. We encourage you to experiment, to give your heart free rein to try things, make mistakes and embrace your work wholeheartedly. Sigmund Freud, the founder of psychoanalysis, explained that the best way for growth to occur in his patients was to let them have the freedom to do what they need to do:

> ... one willingly leaves untouched as much of the patient's personal freedom as is compatible with these restrictions, nor does one hinder him from carrying out unimportant intentions, even if they are foolish; one does not forget that it is in fact only through his own experience and mishaps that a person learns sense.[4]

It is in your personal experience that true integration of heart-centered principles will occur. Ask yourself: "Who among my associates am I avoiding?" "Who irritates me?" "Which of the virtues do I need to practice more completely? Is it commitment to personal growth, open-mindedness, authenticity, trust and detachment, integrity/foresight, humility/humbleness and/or self-care/emotional health?" As the saying goes, "Virtue never tested is no virtue at all."

We think it is appropriate to end this book on the topic of virtues, and to remind readers that we chose these seven virtues because they are core entry points to heart-centered leadership. Thomas Carlyle wrote, "Virtue is like health: the harmony of the whole man."[5] As we said before, the proof will be in your own willingness to work through, to apply the principles, to practice the virtues.

> Better keep yourself clean and bright;
> you are the window through which
> you must see the world.
> —G. B. Shaw (1856-1950)[6]

Chapter Endnotes

1. Carl Gustav Jung Quotes Web site, http://www.phnet.fi/public/
mamaa1/jung.htm.

Introduction

1. This interview with Andy Pearson appears in *Fast Company*
magazine (Dorsey, David. 2001. "Andy Pearson finds love."
Fast Company, August: 78).

2. *Workforce*, October 1997, Vol. 76, Issue 10, p.44.

Chapter 1

1. Elaborating on the research note on page 31, what proof exists
for the claim that a heart-centered leader will become more and
more necessary? A number of companies have been shown to
be successful, partly because they had a philosophy of heart-
centered leadership. For readers who want scientific proof for
heart-centered leadership, we offer a brief review of the literature.
While the scientific studies on leadership are too voluminous
and complex to be reviewed here, many of them suggest that
our ideas are right. We believe the studies reviewed below show
that leaders who an adopt a heartfelt, flexible, and selfless style
of leadership, will be more likely to steer companies to success
in complex times than those who cannot.

   First, Jim Collins describes his research on "Level 5
Leadership" in the *Harvard Business Review* (January 2001). Collins
studied more than 1,400 companies and found that 11 of them
had outstanding and sustained success, with stock returns three
times the rate of the market. The main characteristics of the 11
companies is they had leaders who share certain characteristics:
deep personal humility, intense professional will to do what it
takes to succeed, and the tendency to give credit to others while
assigning blame to themselves. Such humility, self-honesty and
nonjudgmental qualities overlap with the qualities described for
heart-centered leaders. Importantly, these leaders' companies

not only are profitable, they have sustained success and are resilient over time.

Second, Daniel Goleman researched nearly 4,000 executives and examined those who were able to affect the work climate of their organizations. He also obtained financial results from their companies such as return on sales, revenue growth, efficiency and profitability. A core characteristic of these effective leaders is their ability to switch between different leadership styles, fitting themselves to the situation and climate of the organization, in order to obtain results.

Goleman explains that these effective leaders: " … are exquisitely sensitive to the impact they are having on others and seamlessly adjust their style to get the best results. These are leaders, for example, who can read in the first minutes of conversation that a talented but underperforming employee has been demoralized by an unsympathetic, do-it-the-way-I-tell-you manager and needs to be inspired through a reminder of why her work matters. Or that leader might choose to reenergize the employee by asking her about her dreams and aspirations and finding ways to make her job more challenging." Key qualities in these leaders are empathy, flexibility, sensitivity to the situation and a willingness to let go.

Third, leadership scientist Robert House and his colleagues from the University of Pennsylvania conducted an interesting study of American Presidents. These researchers used information from each president's first inaugural address to determine his personality motives.

Two key motives are the need for power and activity inhibition. Need for power is a concern with strong, vigorous action that affects others, action that has an emotional impact on others, and reputation and status. Activity inhibition is the willingness to set aside personal goals for the sake of realizing corporate or institutional goals. Both of these measures are positively and significantly related to different measures of presidential performance (e.g., economic, international and social).

This study shows that presidential effectiveness requires a balance between the drive to influence others and a willingness to set aside personal goals. Findings also show that performance is related to a president's ability to take action that is not necessarily popular. In other words, successful presidents know their impact and have the integrity to follow through, regardless of whether they are liked. House and his colleagues write: "They achieve both positive and negative substantive effects by enacting the power motive and by departing from societal motive norms. Such leaders are transcendental – they transcend the ethos of their times – and make a difference by being different."

In addition to these separate studies, there is a growing body of research literature on the concept of transformational leadership that suggests that transformational leaders may be more effective. Transformational leaders are intellectually stimulating, giving individualized attention and encouragement for different viewpoints within a group; inspiring others to a collective goal and the consideration of the long-term impact of their actions (Bass and Avolio, 1994). Different studies also have shown that transformational leaders are more likely to have subordinates who seek out their ideas, who generate new ideas (Sosik, 1997), and who are satisfied with organizational mergers (Covin & Kelenko, 1997). Such leadership is associated with work unit effectiveness (Lowe, et al, 1996; *Leadership Quarterly*). Finally, there is a growing body of literature on "enlightened management" and financial success. The term "enlightened management" comes from the work of Abraham Maslow, who described the need for management practices to invest in the "human side" of business. Indeed, companies show more profit when they subscribe to any of the following "enlightened" practices.

- Share profits and gains with employees.
- Share information broadly and have broad programs of employee involvement.
- Utilize flexible work designs (flexible hours, job rotation).
- Utilize training and development programs.

References for this endnote:

Bass, B. and B. J. Avolio. "Transformational leadership and organizational culture". *International Journal of Public Administration* 17, no. 3-4 (March 1994): 541-55.

Collins, J. "Level 5 leadership; The triumph of humility and fierce resolve." *Harvard Business Review* 79, no. 1 (January 2001): 67-77.

Goleman, D. "Leadership that gets results." *Harvard Business Review* 78, no. 2 (March 2000): 78-90.

House, R., W. D. Spangler and J. Woycke. "Personality and charisma in the U.S. presidency: A psychological theory of leader effectiveness." *Administrative Science Quarterly* 36, no. 3 (September 1991): 364-397.

Lowe, K. B., K.G. Kroeck and N. Sivasubramaniam. "Effectiveness correlates of transformational and transactional leadership: A meta-analytic review of the MLQ literature." *Leadership Quarterly* 7, issue 3 (Fall 1996): 385-426.

Maslow, Abraham H., Deborah C. Stephens and Gary Heil. 1998. *Maslow on Management.* New York: John Wiley.

Sosik, J.J. "Effects of transformational leadership and anonymity on idea generation in computer-mediated groups." *Group & Organization Management* 22, no. 4 (December 1997): 460-488.

2. This affirmation on page 35 is one of hundreds of positive statements that can be found in the workbooks of "Holographic Repatterning." Holographic Repatterning (HR) is an interactive process for creating positive change and moving clients to higher states of coherence. To learn more about HR visit www.holographic.org. One of the authors of *Heart-Centered Leadership* (Joel) is a practitioner of HR. Various affirmations used in this book have been adapted for HR.

Chapter 2

1. Brussat, Frederic and Mary Ann Brussat. 1998. *Spiritual Literacy: Reading the Sacred in Everyday Life.* Louisville, KY: Touchstone Publishing Co.

2. Brussat, Frederic and Mary Ann Brussat. 2000. *Spiritual Rx: Prescriptions for Living a Meaningful Life.* New York: Hyperion.

Chapter 3

1. The Federal Air Surgeon's Medical Bulletin, Summer 1999 Web site. "Air Rage: Modern-Day Dogfight" (Capt. Donato J. Borrillo, MD, JD), http://www.cami.jccbi.gov/aam- 400a/fasmb/fas9902/airrage.htm.

2. Family Care Gambia – Making a Difference in West Africa Web site, http://familycare.gambianet.com/quotes/people.htm.

Chapter 4

1. Appelbaum, Steven H., Michael Bregman and Peter Moroz. "Fear as a strategy: effects and impact within the organization." *Journal of European Industrial Training* 22, no. 3 (1998): 113-127.

2. Time Online Edition Web site. "Person of the Year 2001" (By Eric Pooley), http://www.time.com/time/poy2001/poyprofile.html.

3. The Johari Window was developed by Joe Luft and Harry Ingham at the University of California in the 1950s and has been used in many courses on communication and leadership development. A seminal reference is *Of Human Interaction* by Joseph Luft (National Press, 1969).

4. Leonard Berry, a leading expert on service quality, profiled the company in his book, *Discovering the Soul of Service: The Nine Drivers of Sustainable Business Success* (Free Press, 1999). We discovered this book through an article by Jennifer Koch Laabs on the Web site, www.workforce.com, an excellent resource for human resource — and business-related articles.

5. From a collection of Zen and tai-chi stories found on the Internet at www.utah.edu/stc.tai-chi/stories.html. Similar stories may be found in *Zen Flesh, Zen Bones: A Collection of Zen and Pre-Zen Writings* by Paul Reps and Nyogen Senzaki (Boston: Shambala Publications, 1994).

Chapter 5

1. Leader to Leader Institute Web site. "The Art of Chaordic Leadership" (by Dee Hock), http://www.pfdf.org/leaderbooks/121/winter2000/hock.html

2. References for this endnote:
   Bennett, Nathan and Christopher L. Martin. "Coping with a layoff: A longitudinal study of victims." *Journal of Management* 21, no. 6 (1995): 1025.
   Cascio, Wayne F. "Downsizing: what do we know? What have we learned?" *The Academy of Management Executive* 7, no. 1 (February 1993): 95.
   Copeland, Tom. "Cutting costs without drawing blood: A framework for boosting profitability without reducing the

headcount." *Harvard Business Review* 78, issue 5 (Sept-Oct 2000): 155.

Skarlicki, Daniel P. and Robert Folger. "When tough times make tough bosses: Managerial distancing as function of layoff blame." *Academy of Management Journal* 41, no. 1 (February 1998): 79

A good resource for articles such as this is the Web site management.about.com.

3. The Ribbon Online Web site, http://www.theribbon.com/poetry/lettinggo.asp.

4. Harvard Business Online Web site, "Don't Hire the Wrong CEO", http://harvardbusinessonline.hbsp.harvard.edu/b02/en/common/item_detail.jhtml?id=8938.

Chapter 6

1. The Warren Buffet Bookshelf Web site, http://www.cyberhaven.com/bookshop/buffettbookshelf.html.

2. Crawford, Fred and Ryan Mathews. 2001. *The Myth of Excellence: Why Great Companies Never Try to be the Best at Everything*. New York: Crown Business. The opposite example, showing how a company fails because it does not follow the principle of "Know your Impact", can be found in a book by Robert Bryce and Molly Ivins, *Pipe Dreams: Greed, Ego and the Death of Enron*. Public Affairs Press (2002).

3. Mathews was quoted in the June 2001 *Fast Company* article by Alan M. Weber – "New rules: Why values beat value" – accessed online at the *Fast Company* Web site: www.fastcompany.com/learning/bookshelf/mathews.html.

4. The exercise is adapted from an article by two management researchers, Sharon K. Parker from the University of New South Wales and Carolyn M. Axtell from the University of Sheffield. We extend their research – which focused on employees and suppliers – to apply to leaders and those they serve, including associates, customers and suppliers. (See: Parker, Sharon K. and Carolyn M. Axtell. "Seeing another viewpoint: Antecedents and outcomes of employee perspective taking." *Academy of Management Journal* 44, no.6 (December 2001):1085.)

5. Robert E. Kaplan, from the Center for Creative Leadership, in his book: Kaplan, Robert E., Wilfred Drath and Joan R. Kofodimos. 1991. *Character Shifts: The Challenge of Improving Executive Performance Through Personal Growth.* London. Jossey-Bass.

6. Bennett, J. B. 1986. "Power and influence in the personality: A psychometric approach." University of Texas at Austin: *Dissertation Abstracts International* 47, 2-B (August 1986): 846. Also see: Bennett, J. "Power and influence as distinct personality traits: Development and validation of a psychometric measure." *Journal of Research in Personality* 22 (September 1988): 361-394.

Chapter 7

1. From Proverbs 16:18 RSV.

2. Maslow, Abraham H., Deborah C. Stephens and Gary Heil. *Maslow on Management.* New York: John Wiley, 1998.

3. Satava, David and Jim Weber. "The ABCs of supervision: Technical skills are only half the story." *Journal of Accountancy* 185, no.2 (February 1998): 72.

4. From Vanekeren, Glen. 1994. *Speakers Sourcebook II: Quotes, Stories & Anecdotes for Every Occasion.* New York: Prentice Hall Press. Used by permission of Perigee Books, an imprint of Penguin Group (USA) Inc.

5. The idea for the list of thoughts from associates was stimulated by our reading the pamphlet *Walk Awhile In My Shoes* by Eric Harvey and Steve Ventura (Dallas: Performance Publishing Company, 1996). The pamphlet is available through The Walk The Talk Company (www.walkthetalk.com) – we recommend their tools as helpful aids for heart-centered leadership.

6. From Helminkski, Camille and Kabir Helminski. *Rumi Daylight: A Daybook of Spiritual Guidance.* Boston: Shambhala Publications Inc., 1999.

7. Josephson Institute of Ethics Web site, "Simplicity, Humility," http://www.josephsoninstitute.org/quotes/quotesimplicity.htm

8. Tangney, J. P. "Humility: Theoretical perspectives, empirical findings and directions for future research." *Journal of Social and Clinical Psychology* 19, no.1 (2000): 70-82.

Chapter 8

1. From an interview with Ron Chernow in Business Week Online, November 8, 2001. Chernow is author of *Titan: The Life of John D. Rockefeller* (New York: Random House, 1998).

2. Malone, Michael. "Killer Results Without Killing Yourself." *Fast Company*, no.1 (November 1995): 124.

3. Ornish, Dean. *Love & Survival: The Scientific Basis for the Healing Power of Intimacy*. With foreword by Andrew Weil, M.D. New York: HarperCollins, 1998.

4. Pert, Candace B. *Molecules of Emotion: Why You Feel the Way You Feel*. With foreword by Deepak Chopra, M.D. New York: Touchstone, 1997.

5. Pearsall, Paul. *The Heart's Code: Tapping the Wisdom and Power of Our Heart Energy*. New York: Random House, 1998.

6. The Heartmath Solution – Institute of Heartmath Web site, http://heartmath.org.

7. Pearsall, P., G. E. Schwartz and L. G. Russek. "Changes in heart transplant recipients that parallel the personalities of their donors." *Integrative Medicine* 2, no.2 (March 21, 2000): 65:72. Also see: Pearsall, P. K. "Are heart transplant recipients receiving cellular memories from their donated organ? A heuristic study." *Hawaii Medical Journal* 60, no.11 (November 2001): 282, 300.

8. Ornish, *Love & Survival: The Scientific Basis for the Healing Power of Intimacy*.

9. Quick, J. C., J. H. Gavin, C. L. Cooper and J. D. Quick. "Executive health: building strengths, managing risks." *Academy of Management Executive* 14, no.2 (2000): 34-44. Also see "Stress, the Business Traveler and Corporate Health: An International Travel Health Symposium," April 27-28, 2000, The World Bank, Washington D.C.; Gilbert, B." The myths and realities of executive health." *Management Magazine*, no. 7 (August 1993): 8-10.

10. From "Executive health: building strengths, managing risks." (Quick, Gavin, Cooper and Quick, p. 37-8),

11. Ganster, D. C., J. Schaubroeck, W. E. Sime and B. T. Mayes. "Unhealthy leader dispositions, work group strain and performance." *Academy of Management Proceedings*, (1990) p. 191-6.

12. Bernin, P., T. Theorell and C. G. Sandberg. "Biological correlates of social support and pressure at work in managers." *Integrative Physiological & Behavioral Science* 36, no.3 (July-September 2001): 121-137.

    Also see: Richard, P. and J. Siegrist. "Chronic work stress, sickness, absence and hypertension in middle managers: general or specific." *Social Science & Medicine* 45, no.7 (October 1997): 1111-1121.

13. A list of risk calculators is available at the "What you need to know about" Web site (http://heartdisease.about.com/cs/riskcalculators). These calculators require knowledge of your cholesterol levels and blood pressure.

14. Following is a list of books that provide more facts and research on various complementary and alternative therapies:
    Shannon, S. *Handbook of Complementary and Alternative Therapies in Mental Health*. San Diego: Academic Press, 2002.
    Trivieri, L. *The American Holistic Medical Association Guide to Holistic Health: Healing Therapies*. New York: John Wiley, 2001.
    Brody, J. E. and D. Grady. *New York Times Guide to Alternative Health*. New York: Henry Holt, 2001.
    Novey, D. W. *Clinician's Complete Reference to Complementary/Alternative Medicine*. St. Louis: Mosby-Year Book, 2000.
    Jonas, W. B. and J. S. Levin, Eds. *Essentials of Complementary and Alternative Medicine*. Philadelphia: Lippincott Williams & Wilkins, 1999.
    Pelletier, K. and A. Weil. *Best Alternative Medicine*. Fireside, 2002.

15. See H. G. Koenig, M. E. McCullough and D. B. Larson. *Handbook of Religion and Health*. Oxford University Press, 2000; H. G. Koenig. *Handbook of Religion and Health*. Academic Press, 1998; and Levin, J. and L. Dossey. *God, Faith, and Health: Exploring the Spirituality-Healing Connection*. New York: John Wiley, 2001.

16. This list is adapted from "How Your Heart Works" by Carl Bianco, M.D. (www.howstuffworks.com/heart.htm).

17. Adapted from "Listening with the ear of the heart (achieving unity of mind and heart to gain spirituality)," *CrossCurrents* (Spring 1999), by Frank T. Griswold.

18. There are many references to the relationship between heart and religious faith in both the Old and New Testament. Interested readers may look at the Web site of preacher Roy Allen Davison and read "Is the Word of God written on your heart?" (www.oldpaths.com/Archive/Davison/Roy/Allen/1940/home.html). For a historical discussion of the "sacred heart" in Roman Catholicism see www.wikipedia.org/wiki/Sacred_Heart. An on-line Catholic encyclopedia also provides a doctrinal explanation (see www.newadvent.org/cathen/07163a.htm).

19. Information about Taoism was gathered from several Web sites: www.taoism.net; www.geocities.com/tao4dummies/; and www.nauticom.net/www/asti/dao_jing.htm

20. From the *Tao Te Ching* by Lao Tzu (translated by Gia-Fu Feng and Jane English, New York: Knopf, 1972).

21. Quoted in *Meditations with Mechtild of Magdeburg*, edited by Sue Woodruff (Santa Fe: Bear & Co., 1982).

Chapter 9

1. The Quotations Page Web site, http://www.quotationspage.com/quote/25850.html

2. Janet Hagberg. *Real Power: Stages of Personal Power in Organizations.* Salem, WI: Sheffield Publishing, Co, 1994.

3. Virtue, Innocence and Purity Web site, http://www.quotations.com/virtue.htm

4. Ariga Web site, http://www.ariga.com/frosties/freudsigmund.shtml

5. theotherpages Web site, http://www.theotherpages.org/unsort01.html

6. The People's Cyber Nation Web site, http://www.cyber-nation.com/victory/quotations/authors/quotes_shaw_georgebernard.html

Heart-Centered Leadership: Seven Principles and Corresponding Values

By Susan Steinbrecher and Joel B. Bennett, Ph.D.

Principle	Virtue (Emotion to Resonate With)
Know Thyself *Definition: Ongoing willingness to look in the mirror and assess one's own strengths as well as one's personal opportunities for growth*	**Commitment to Personal Growth** *Antidote to: Blaming, projecting problems on others, pointing the finger, lack of internal accountability*
Don't Assume, Don't Judge, Come to Understand *Definition: Willingness to assume associates have a positive intention and, accordingly, give them the benefit of the doubt; willingness to explore and engage with others; appreciative inquiry*	**Open-Mindedness** *Antidote to: Being judgmental, closed thinking, rushing to judgment based on limited data, focusing only on your own view, lack of perspective*
They Need What You Need *Definition: Understanding that we are not separate and not really different from our associates; we are all human with similar physical, mental, and spiritual needs*	**Authenticity** *Antidote to: Manipulativeness, lack of perspective, lack of discernment of truth, dissembling, protecting corporate and self image at all costs*
Letting Go *Definition: Trusting associates; trusting that things happen for a reason; having faith in the process*	**Detachment** *Antidote to: Controlling, pushing outcomes, dominating solutions*
Know the Impact of Your Words and Actions *Definition: Being in tune with and having a healthy respect for the impact of the leader; being mindful of how words and actions may be interpreted in formal and informal ways*	**Integrity/Foresight** *Antidote to: Impulsiveness, short-range thinking, lack of moral compass, failure to appreciate the awesome responsibility afforded to leadership*
Associates Have a Choice—They Ultimately Will Go Along or Not *Definition: Recognition that associates have a choice at mental and emotional levels as well as in behavior; recognition that associate compliance does not always equate with emotional engagement*	**Humility/Humbleness** *Antidote to: Arrogance, belief that position power is "real" power, egoistic striving for power, grandiosity, narcissism, discounting the value and needs of associates*
Care for the Heart *Definition: Recognition that one's whole self must stay healthy in order to live the principles; includes emotional and spiritual as well as physical health; appreciation of how one models health to associates*	**Self-Care/Emotional Health** *Antidote to: Unhealthy lifestyle and poor health habits (diet, exercise, rest, stress management); lack of spiritual perspective and meaningfulness at work (e.g., ethics and inspiration)*